CONVENTIONAL GEAR

GEAR

Flying A Taildragger

CONVENTIONAL GEAR

Flying A Taildragger

DAVID ROBSON

A Focus Series Book
Aviation Supplies & Acadamics, Inc
Newcastle, Washington

Conventional Gear: Flying A Taildragger
by David P. Robson

First published 2001 ASA.

Aviation Supplies & Academics, Inc.
7005 132nd Place SE
Newcastle, Washington 98059-3153
Email: asa@asa2fly.com
Website: www.asa2fly.com

Published 2001 by Aviation Supplies & Academics, Inc.

Acknowledgments:
Fred Boyns for the title. John Freeman, Captain John Laming, David Pilkington, Tom
Russel and Peter Whellum for sharing their lifetimes of taildragging experience and
Rod Irvine for the Storch check rides.

Photographs:
Lincoln: Captain John Laming
Drover, Chipmunk, C185 and CAP10: Garry Veroude
Southern Cross Replica, Lincoln and Dakota: Royal Australian Air Force

Graphics and Layout:
Aviation Theory Centre, Melbourne, Australia

Printed in the United States of America

2017   2016   2015   2014   2013   7   6   5   4

ASA-CON-GEAR
ISBN 1-56027-460-3
     978-1-56027-460-5

Library of Congress Cataloging-in-Publication Data
Robson, David
     Conventional gear : flying a taildragger/David Robson.
          p.   cm.
        "A focus series book."
        ISBN 1–56027–460–3
        1. Taildragger airplanes — Piloting. I. Title.
     TL711.T28 R63   2001
     629.132'5243—dc21   2001053578

Table of Contents

Part Two: Flight Techniques

Part 3: Some Different Taildraggers

Author/Editor

David Robson is a career aviator, having been nurtured on balsa wood, dope (the legal kind) and tissue paper. He made his first solo flight in a de Havilland Chipmunk shortly after his seventeenth birthday. He had made his first parachute jump at age sixteen. His first job was as a junior draftsman at the Commonwealth Aircraft Corporation in Melbourne, Australia. At the same time, he continued flying lessons with the Royal Victorian Aero Club. He joined the Royal Australian Air Force (RAAF) in 1965, and served for twenty-one years as a fighter pilot and test pilot. He flew over 1,000 hours on Mirages and 500 on Sabres (F-86 with a Rolls-Royce engine). He completed the Empire Test Pilot's course at Boscombe Down in England in 1972, flying everything from gliders to the magnificent Hunter, Canberra and Lightning. He completed a tour in Vietnam with the United States Air Force as a forward air controller, flying the O-2A (*Oscar Deuce*). He was a member of the seven-aircraft formation aerobatic team, the Deltas, which flew his favorite aircraft, the Mirage fighter. This team was specially formed to celebrate the fiftieth anniversary of the RAAF.

David Robson has been flying taildraggers for more than forty years. He first learned to fly in the de Havilland Chipmunk and the Australian Air Force CAC Winjeel. He continued to fly the Winjeel throughout his career as a fighter pilot and FAC. As a test pilot, he flew the Chipmunk, Dakota and Twin Pioneer.

After leaving the air force he became a flight instructor and spent time teaching spinning, aerobatics and landings in the Citabria and Decathlon. He also instructed in the Maule. He has flown some very special antique airplanes including the Auster, Tiger Moth, Aeronca, Beech Staggerwing and the wonderful Drover.

He completed John Freeman's low-level safety course in the Cessna 185. More recently, as development manager of the Australian Aviation College, where he regularly taught aerobatics and tail wheel operations, he introduced the CAP 10B to Australia. In the past two years he has been introduced to ultralights, flying the Drifter and the Storch.

One day he would love to fly what is, for him, the ultimate taildragger: the A-1 Skyraider.

Contributors to Part Three

Peter Whellum

Peter has been flying since 1975 and has been involved in commercial aviation since 1980, including service with the S.A. Police Airwing and later as chief pilot for a large outback tourist organization. He has a long-term commitment to improving flight training standards throughout general aviation, with particular interest and personal involvement in the development of computer-based training and testing, and in aviation multimedia development. He is a member of the Antique Aeroplane Association and an owner of an Auster J/1N that knows its own way around outback Australia.

John Freeman

John Freeman has been a pilot for fifty years in arguably the most dangerous field of aviation: agricultural flying. He has conducted agricultural flight operations in Europe, Africa, China and throughout Australia, including night operations. He began in Tiger Moths and has flown most agricultural aircraft including the very powerful turbine-powered Thrush. He started his own agricultural business, Trojan Aerial Services, with his own aircraft including Tiger Moths, Piper Pawnees, Super Cubs, and a Cessna 185 which alternated between floats and wheels. John became, in turn, the aviation authority examiner of airmen for agricultural operations for eleven years and wrote the manual on agricultural flying. Over the past 25 years he has taught many agricultural pilots the correct (safe) way to operate. He has since developed a low-level safety awareness course for all pilots to improve safety standards near the ground. He has devoted his full-time attention to this project since 1992.

Captain John Laming

John is justifiably proud of his aviation career that spans more than 50 years. John served with the Royal Australian Air Force, the Civil Aviation Safety Authority and four major airlines. John has flown a wide variety of aircraft including Mustangs (P-51), Vampires, Lincoln bombers, DC-3s and Boeing 737s. He was awarded the Air Force Cross in 1962 and attained the rank of Squadron Leader (Lieutenant-Colonel) before leaving the Air Force in 1969 to fly as a civilian pilot. John lives in Melbourne, Australia, and is a Boeing 737 simulator instructor. He likes to write aviation articles in his spare time.

Captain Don Hutchinson

Captain Don Hutchinson has had 46 years' involvement in aviation as an instructor, charter pilot, airline pilot, theory instructor and technical writer. He has logged 11,000 hours, flying both fixed- and rotary-wing aircraft, including the tail wheel types of the Auster, Tiger Moth, Chipmunk, Cessna 185 and DC-3. Other airplane types include the DC-4, F27, F28, ATR42 and DC-9. Helicopter types flown are the Bell Model 47, Bell Model 206, Robinson R22 and Hughes 500.

David Pilkington

David Pilkington has been in the aviation industry since 1966 when he started flying as an aeronautical engineering student at RMIT, then at Cranfield College of Aeronautics. He has held a variety of positions including chief aerodynamicist and designer on the Nomad and Wamira projects. His flying interests are purely aerobatic: he has been an Australian Advanced Aerobatic Champion, a Pitts aerobatic formation team member, a low-level aerobatic testing officer, and an aerobatic instructor. His flying and engineering interests were combined for the development of the Laser. In 1995, he joined Aviat in the US as vice-president of engineering, and as test/demonstration pilot for the new Pitts and the Husky. David has since returned to Melbourne, where he worked for Boeing Australia and lately British Aerospace Australia as an engineer. He moonlights on weekends as a flight instructor, teaching aerobatics in anything from the Cessna Aerobat to the Pitts S-2A, in between wringing out his Laser. He is now the proud owner of a Decathlon.

Captain Tom Russel

Tom began his aviation career as an air cadet and was promoted to become an officer in the RAAF Reserve (ANG) where, to this day, he teaches multi-crew cooperation in the Lockheed P-3 flight simulator. He began commercial flying as a flight instructor and then progressed through the normal path of charter operations until joining a regional airline. Later he joined a major Australian airline that pioneered scheduled flight operations in Papua New Guinea, which is probably the most difficult country for flight operations in the entire world due to its severe tropical weather, blind valleys, one-way short sloping airstrips and mountainous terrain.

He commanded DC-3s, Fokker F27s and F28s, and was heavily involved in the check and training of both expatriate pilots and the national pilot training program. Tom was directly involved in the introduction of PNG night operations and international routes for the F28s.

On return to Australia, he joined the Department of Aviation as a Flight Examiner of both GA and RPT pilots. He became involved in the introduction of new airplane types, which necessitated a great deal of hands-on flying and training of new check captains.

Due to his flight time on DC-3s, he was also seconded to be the project flight examiner for the Southern Cross Replica project. This became a very hands-on active role in forming the necessary regulatory framework for the training and checking of flight crews on an aircraft that represented a 50-year-old design and did not comply with modern RPT regulations and design requirements. He later became the senior flight testing officer of airline cadet pilots at the Australian Aviation College, mainly being involved with the Cathay Finesse (CRM) program and multi-crew training of Chinese cadets in a Beech C90 King Air. Tom is currently enjoying his role as captain of a Jetstream commuter airplane on regional routes in Southern Australia.

Introduction

As the old hand once said, "taildraggers teach tight technique."

In times past, the standard configuration for an airplane's landing gear was the tail wheel—two main wheels and a smaller tail wheel at the rear of the fuselage.

This was standard. Conventional aircraft landed on airfields that were literally fields without defined sealed runways, just dusty, grassy, soggy or boggy ground. Airplanes landed into the wind (as is best) and difficulties with crosswinds were not significant. (The nose wheel, which had been considered many years before, would not have survived for long on the soft ground.)

The tail wheel configuration was lighter, presented less drag and was less vulnerable to uneven ground and soft patches. It also forced the pilot to cross the threshold at the right speed, so that the airplane arrived in the correct attitude for landing. As airplane speeds increased, fixed gear was replaced by retractable mains (partly retracting on the DC-3 and fully enclosed on fighters). Eventually, even the tail wheel retracted, but still the standard configuration was tail wheel.

Then came the war. Aircraft needed to carry more fuel and bombs, in all weather conditions. They needed longer runways and could not tolerate soft, wet grass. These higher-performance airplanes needed sealed runways that were not always (hardly ever) aligned to the prevailing wind. The tricycle landing gear (nose wheel in front) was easier to control in a crosswind and the sealed runway removed the threat of nose wheel collapse (except for during a mishandled takeoff or landing when wheelbarrowing could occur). The tricycle configuration replaced the conventional gear. I believe the B-29 was the first bomber, and the P-38 and P-39 were the first fighters, to have tricycle gear.

Flying a tail wheel aircraft demanded accurate airspeed control (for the aircraft to stay on the ground after touchdown) and smooth technique (to arrive in the correct landing attitude, to maintain attitude and directional control on and near the ground and to touch the ground gently enough to control the reaction). This discipline is required in a tricycle aircraft, but to a lesser degree: they are more tolerant (more forgiving of inaccuracies and lazy feet), and we humans like it easy.

Jets reinforced the demise of the tail wheel for several reasons:
- they needed even longer runways;
- jet efflux tore up or melted the bitumen runways (so aircraft had to be level on the ground); and
- the jet encouraged laziness as there was no engine torque and therefore no lateral/directional trim change with thrust/power changes, the rudder becoming almost redundant.

Simultaneously, more complex flight controls removed adverse aileron yaw. Rudder pedals became mere footrests. Thus we have allowed a laxity in piloting accuracy.

As a result, there has developed a strong argument for the retention of a tail wheel aircraft in the curriculum for primary flight training. Poor handling of the flare and touchdown, inaccurate speed control and inadequate crosswind technique are common faults. Today, some experienced pilots have not been correctly trained and disciplined in their primary flight school as they have not had to cope with a taildragger.

Devotees of taildraggers claim other advantages such as shorter takeoff and landing distances. Does the taildragger takeoff or land in a shorter distance? In theory, no. If both aircraft have the same power, same liftoff speed, same takeoff weight, correct threshold speed, same landing weight, the same touchdown speed and the same braking, they should take off or stop in the same distance. But, because the nose wheel configuration is more forgiving, there is a tendency to carry extra speed and to accept less precise or less positive control.

Some modern aircraft also have limited elevator power (to prevent stalling) so have to touch down faster or keep power on. In the case of a tail wheel airplane, a wheeler landing requires some additional speed and therefore additional landing distance.

The tail wheel is a more challenging aircraft to fly well and offers far more fun and interest. It is eminently more satisfying to land well. Hence, the strong following for antiques and warbirds. It would not be nearly as interesting if they were all tricycle configured.

Ultralights, homebuilts, aerobatic and agricultural aircraft retain conventional gear for the same reasons that made it most common in the first place: it is lighter, less complex, less draggy and less vulnerable on soft ground. Besides, it's more fun. Every pilot should fly a taildragger at least once in their career. There is no more satisfying feeling than a greaser, a three-point landing on soft grass as the tires brush the blades of grass and the hiss of the wheels signals a perfect touchdown.

Welcome to the challenging and fun world of conventional gear.

Part One

Theory

Chapter 1

The Tail Wheel Airplane

The standard configuration of the landing gear on airplanes prior to and during World War II was the tail wheel. The tricycle configuration was progressively introduced with sealed runways. To differentiate the two, the tail wheel configuration became known as *conventional gear*. These days, it is commonly called a *tail wheel configuration* or *taildragger*. Tricycle gear is sometimes abbreviated to *trike*.

In terms of general aircraft structure, the taildragger is little different from a tricycle configuration. However, the differences are important as they affect aircraft behavior and pilot control techniques. Further, the control finesse needed for a taildragger, especially in crosswind conditions, is affected by the particular airplane design. While you may have a tail wheel rating, you should also have a specific dual check ride for each taildragger that you fly, as they can vary very much in behavior.

Taildraggers come in many shapes and sizes:

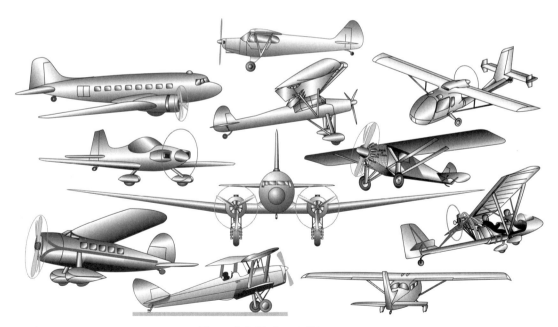

Figure 1-1. Various taildraggers.

The major assemblies of the airplane are the:
- fuselage;
- wings;
- empennage (tail surfaces);
- flight and ancillary control surfaces;
- landing gear (undercarriage);
- engine and propeller; and
- systems (such as fuel and electrical systems).

Airplane Design Features

When we consider taildraggers, we must recognize that the characteristics of many taildraggers are the same as any small, light, low-powered, fabric-covered airplane, regardless of their landing gear configuration.

Low-Inertia Aircraft

You will hear the expression *low-inertia aircraft* to describe lightweight, draggy designs, such as many ultralights and traditional types like Cubs and Tiger Moths. It simply means that, due to low mass and high drag, the airplane has a much less tendency to maintain flight path and airspeed. Therefore, with engine failure, the pilot has little time in which to react, and so must lower the nose positively, severely and immediately to maintain airspeed and control.

Wing Loading

The wing loading of the airplane is the ratio of its weight to its wing area. The lower the wing loading, the lower the stalling airspeed, and the more it will respond to gusts of wind (it is trickier in a crosswind). The clipped-wing Cub rides better than the standard Cub because it has a reduced wing area for the same weight, but it also stalls at a higher airspeed.

Gust Response

An airplane will respond to vertical wind gusts and thermals depending on its wing loading and the shape of the airfoil (its change of lift coefficient with angle of attack). A light airplane with a high-lift airfoil will respond quickly and positively to a vertical gust whereas a heavy, high-speed warbird will ride the winds with hardly a tremor.

Airplane Structure

Fuselage

The fuselage forms the protective cabin and the connecting structure of the airplane to which the wings, empennage, engine and landing gear are attached. It contains seats for the pilot and passengers, plus the cockpit controls and instruments.

The fuselage of many modern training aircraft is of a semi-monocoque construction, being a light framework covered by a load-bearing skin (usually aluminum). It is a compromise in which the internal framework carries most of the stress, with the remainder being carried by the skin—hence *semi*-monocoque. A monocoque structure is one where the skin carries the total load—like an eggshell. They are light and strong, but very fragile if damaged.

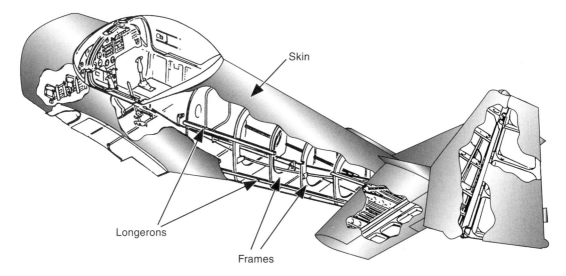

Figure 1-2. Semi-monocoque construction.

Alternatively, many tail wheel aircraft and ultralights have a welded steel-tube fuselage structure, with either an uncovered open lattice or a fabric covering. The wings may also be fabric covered, in which case the skins carry no structural loads (neither bending nor torsion), but do transfer the lift and drag pressures to the primary structure within the wing.

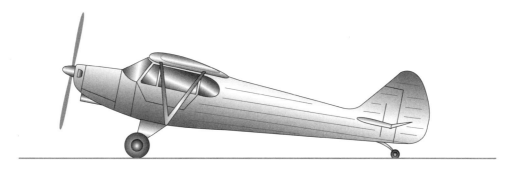

Figure 1-3. Typical taildragger structure.

Wings

The wings generate the lifting force that enables the aircraft to overcome gravity and to maneuver. The wings and their attachments are exposed to heavy loads in maneuvers and turbulence. These loads may be several times the total weight of the airplane. Under FAA regulations (14 CFR Part 23), the airplane structure is designed to accept at least +3.8G (3.8 times its normal, level-flight load) for a normal category airplane.

Wings have one or more internal spars (beams) attached to the fuselage and extending to the wing tips. The spars carry the major loads, both bending (due to turbulence and maneuvering) and twisting (due mainly to control surface deflections).

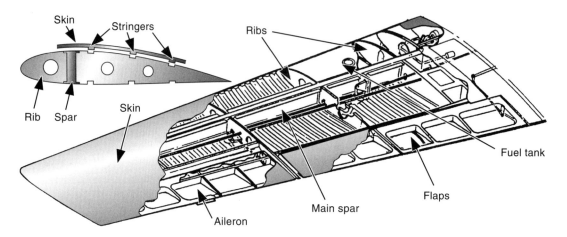

Figure 1-4. Spars, ribs and stringers in the wing.

Ribs, perpendicular to the spar(s), assisted by stringers running parallel to the spars, provide the airfoil shape and stiffen the skin. The ribs transmit the air loads from the skin to the spar(s), and thereby the air carries the weight of the total aircraft. The skin may be aluminum, plywood, composite honeycomb or fabric. All are load-carrying in transferring the pressure differential of the passing air, but only the plywood, composite fiber or aluminum skins add to the structural strength and stiffness of the wings.

Some aircraft have external struts (rigid and able to accept tension and compression loads) or bracing wires (tension only) to provide extra strength by carrying some of the wing loads to the fuselage and relieving some of the bending moment on the spars, especially the wing root attachment (figure 1-5).

An underwing strut can carry the flight loads (in tension) and the ground loads (in compression), which flying wires cannot do. The Cessna series of single-engine aircraft uses this underwing strut configuration.

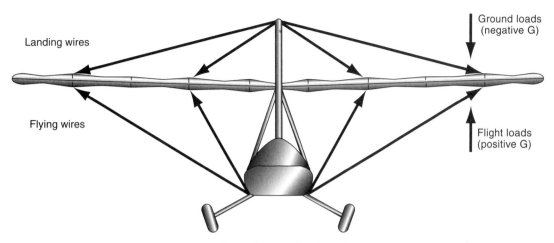

Figure 1-5. External bracing wires.

The low-wing airplane can utilize an overwing strut to carry flight loads in compression and ground loads in tension, such as with the Piper Pawnee. This is not such an efficient arrangement (because long slender pieces cope with tension better than compression), but it still reduces the wing-root bending moments.

The strut attachment points, both to the wings and fuselage, are particularly important and should be inspected regularly for damage, loosened bolts and corrosion. There have been in-flight failures of these critical components.

Many modern aircraft are constructed of composites (glass fiber, carbon fiber, plastics, paper and honeycomb), offering very light and strong structures, without the limitations of metal fatigue. Fatigue is the work hardening, or brittleness, that results in the weakening of a metal subject to repeated bending cycles.

Empennage

The empennage or tail assembly is structurally similar to the wing and consists of a fixed horizontal stabilizer and movable elevators. The horizontal stabilizer may be attached to the side of the fuselage or attached to the top of the vertical stabilizer or fin (called a T-tail). At the rear of the vertical stabilizer is a movable rudder. In some aircraft, the complete horizontal stabilizer and elevator assembly is combined as one movable stabilator.

The rudder and elevators of a taildragger are usually larger than those on a tricycle airplane because the pilot needs more pitch and directional control at low airspeeds and on the ground. Sometimes the space between the movable surface and the fixed stabilator is sealed with a flexible strip to improve effectiveness.

Landing Gear

The landing gear (undercarriage) supports the weight of the airplane when it is on the ground, and carries the vertical stresses (heavy landing), longitudinal stresses (braking and skidding) and lateral stresses (sideloads) on takeoff and landing. It is the most obvious difference between the trike and the taildragger, and it is important to look a little more closely at the design and operation of the landing gear and brakes.

The advantages of a tail wheel configuration are:
- lighter weight;
- reduced drag;
- greater maneuverability in confined spaces on the ground;
- potentially reduced stopping distance; and
- no nose wheel so less vulnerability to damage on unprepared strips

But all this comes at a cost: the taildragger sacrifices ease of directional control in crosswind conditions.

Main Gear Assemblies

Main gear assemblies come in one of several main types:
- spring steel (Cessna) or rubber blocks in compression, or bungees in tension (Cubs and Austers); and
- oleo-pneumatic struts (found on most retractables, warbirds and antiques and many low-wing trainers such as the Piper Warrior).

Rubber or spring-steel assemblies are simple, light and easy to maintain, but there is no damping; that is, there is no component to reduce bounces. They rely on aerodynamics and pilot inputs to control touchdown impact and bounces.

The oleo-pneumatic strut has an oil-and-gas-filled strut, where the gas acts in compression as a spring, and the oil passes through a metered hole to dampen the bounces, like the shock absorber on a car. A long-stroke strut softens the touchdown and reduces bounces (as with the Storch, for example).

Main Wheel Tires

The contact between the aircraft and the ground is primarily via the main wheel tires. (The tail wheel tire has some influence when there is weight upon it.) The condition and pressure of the tires is vital to control on the ground in both braking and steering.

Tire pressure is important as it determines the contact area and the stiffness of the tire. Too little pressure leads to squashy contact with poor braking and steering. Too much pressure leads to a firm ride, too much bounce, and skidding due to reduced contact area.

Depth of tread determines grip for steering and braking, as well as shedding water. Worn tires are a high risk. Creep marks show any relative movement between the wheel and the tire, and indicate if excessive braking has been used, or the airplane has been landed with locked wheels. It is important to check for creep on tires with a separate inner tube as the membrane and the valve could be damaged.

Always report and annotate the maintenance record of any heavy landing and any landings with severe sideloads or ground loops. In some aircraft, stresses to the landing gear attachment points can transfer serious loads and cause damage to the main spar. A heavy landing or a landing with severe sideloads can weaken the entire structure. There have been in-flight break-ups following landing gear or spar damage that was not reported or not properly repaired.

Brakes

Wheel brakes are more important to a taildragger than other aircraft as they are an important part of ground control, not just for stopping, but for steering, especially in confined spaces, and for maintaining directional control in a crosswind.

Brake controls also come in several forms:
• toe brakes that are either a complete pedal that depresses, or a small supplementary pedal above the rudder bar or footrest (CAP 10B);
• heel brakes (Cubs and Austers) that are operated by the pilot's heel;
• a hand lever used in conjunction with rudder bar deflection (Chipmunk); and
• a hand-operated brake lever independent of the rudder (some pneumatic brake systems), usually mounted on the control yoke.

Care Of Brakes

Brakes should be used as the second stage of control for steering; that is, steer first with rudder and tail wheel steering, and then add individual brake pressure to supplement other inputs when necessary. For tight maneuvering, a touch of brake is used to *declutch* the tail wheel and allow it to fully caster. A burst of throttle to improve air over the rudder then allows very tight turns.

When taxiing, make a conscious effort to avoid inadvertent brake pressure, or too much power that then necessitate the use of brakes to control speed.

Pause between heavy applications of brake by taxiing forward with brakes off to allow cooling air to pass over the disk.

Parking Brakes

Some airplanes have a facility to retain brake pressure in the hydraulic lines or cables, and so function as a parking brake. These may have a knob or handle for this purpose. Many taildraggers have no parking brake.

Never trust parking brakes when leaving the aircraft unoccupied or for hand starting. Use chocks or tie-downs. Do not leave the parking brake applied after heavy wheel braking and when brake disks and pads are hot.

Figure 1-6. External steerable
tail wheel with spring centering.

Tail Wheel Assemblies

There are several forms of tail wheel assembly:
- housed in the rudder that always steers and therefore are not centering or locking;
- external castering with neither centering nor locking;
- retractable castering with pin centering when aligned (the Spitfire, for example);
- external castering with manual-locking to central; and
- external steerable via rudder pedals with spring centering to rudder rather than aircraft centerline.

Most tail wheels are mounted on springs or oleos, but some are rigidly connected to the airframe and only steer.

Tail wheels, and their connecting rods or cables, are subject to severe vibrations and can fatigue quickly. They are also susceptible to jamming by grass and dirt. All are susceptible to corrosion and should be kept clean and oiled.

Tail Wheel Tire

The tail wheel tire may be inflatable or, in smaller aircraft, solid rubber.

Tail Skid

Some older aircraft, designed to operate on grass, but not sealed taxiways, have a steerable or trailing skid. This is sprung and functions as a dragging, braking, straightening and steering force. The original Tiger Moth had a skid. On a grass field, it works beautifully to slow and straighten the airplane. In fact, the aircraft is easier to control with a skid than with a tail wheel. However, for operations on sealed runways, the airplane needs a tail wheel, and so also needs wheel brakes.

Chapter 2

Ground and Flight Dynamics

It is invaluable to understand why the taildragger behaves differently from a trike. With this understanding, we can learn and practice how best to anticipate, cope, counter, manage and control the airplane in flight and on ground.

Fundamentally, when the aircraft is totally airborne, there is no difference in behavior between a taildragger and a trike. It is when the wheels are in contact with the ground that things change. First, the center of gravity (CG) of the taildragger wants to raise the nose (increase the angle of attack) instead of reducing the angle of attack. The tail wheel aircraft also wants to deviate from a straight line instead of returning to a straight path.

Ground Dynamics

Geometry (CG Position in Relation to the Main Wheels)

The significant difference between a taildragger and a trike is the position of the CG in relation to the main wheels. This fact causes a situation where any deviation away from a straight line tends to increase rather than decrease. If not caught early, this deviation becomes more rapid and tighter, and the aircraft will ultimately tighten to the extent that it could skid sideways, strike a wing tip, or perhaps slide backwards along its original path.

What happens?

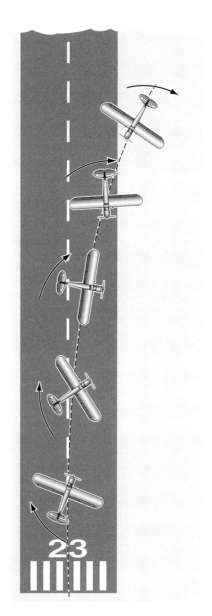

Figure 2-1. Deviation away from straight tends to escalate if not corrected early.

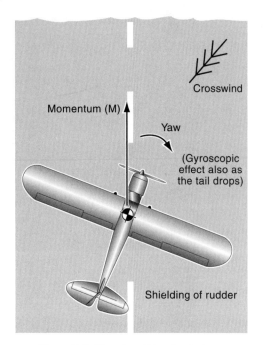

Figure 2-2. The aircraft begins to turn.

When moving forward, the aircraft starts to deviate right due to, say, a wind gust or uneven ground.

If the pilot does not immediately correct this, the momentum of the aircraft tends to maintain its original path, and the difference in drag between the wheels tends to tighten the turn.

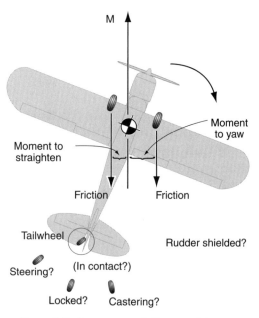

Figure 2-3. If uncorrected, the turn tightens.

The further the turn tightens, the more the deviation winds up. The rate of turn increases and the momentum causes the aircraft to skid sideways. The wing tip may strike the ground. The tail wheel mechanism (locked, steerable, or castering) is significant.

Figure 2-4. The deviation escalates.

The momentum of the turn may cause the aircraft to spin all the way around and slide backward.

If the aircraft passes over slippery gravel, or if one wheel passes through grass or dry contact, the difference in friction between the wheels will increase or counter the turn—we could be lucky or unlucky.

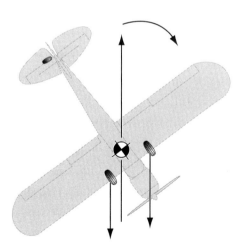

Figure 2-5. The aircraft may even spin right around.

Ground Loop on Takeoff

The takeoff situation is significant in two respects:

- there is high power and therefore powerful slipstream over the rudder so the pilot has maximum control power; and
- the high power and low forward speed increases the number of factors trying to cause the aircraft to deviate.

There is little time for the pilot to react but, when he or she does, there is plenty of response from the rudder.

Dynamic and Aerodynamic Effects of Propellers

All single-engine aircraft have directional problems because of the inbalance of forces caused by the propeller rotation. The very powerful piston-engine fighters with massive propellers are very difficult to control during takeoff and at low flying speed. Training aircraft are easier, but the effects are still noticeable.

There are four effects, all of which try to deviate the aircraft from a straight line and all operate in the same direction. If the engine rotates in a clockwise direction when viewed from the cockpit, then these effects all try to yaw the aircraft to the left. All act when the power is applied except the gyroscopic precession, which only comes into play as the tail is raised. Crosswind can be chosen to offset or aggravate the effect of these problems: if the runway can be chosen to have a crosswind from the right then it will counter the effects.

The four effects are:

- slipstream effect;
- torque reaction;
- gyroscopic precession; and
- asymmetric blade effect.

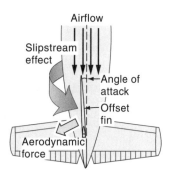

Figure 2-6. An offset fin helps counteract propeller slipstream effect.

Slipstream Effect

A propeller rotating clockwise (as seen from the cockpit) will impart a clockwise rotation to the slipstream as it flows back over the airplane. In the case of a single-engine aircraft, this causes an asymmetric flow over the rear fuselage, fin and rudder. In a twin, the flow is less marked and the effect can be completely self-canceling if the engines rotate in opposite directions. In our case, the slipstream generates an aerodynamic force that pushes the tail to the right and yaws the nose to the left.

Some aircraft have an offset fin or slightly offset engine to help overcome this effect. Otherwise, the pilot has to compensate with rudder.

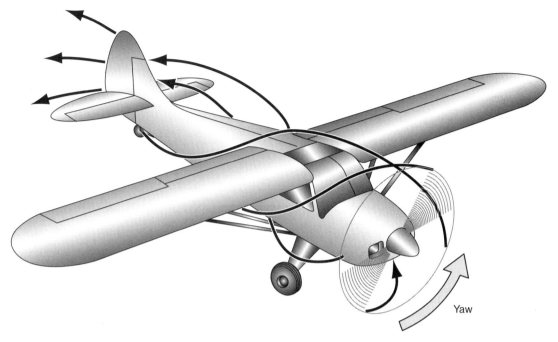

Figure 2-7. Slipstream effect.

Torque Reaction

When the propeller is rotated by the engine, there is an opposing reaction on the engine which, of course, is attached to the aircraft. Thus there is a force trying to rotate the aircraft in the opposite direction to the propeller rotation. This force is directly equal and opposite to the torque applied to the propeller—that is, the higher the power, the higher the torque, and the greater the reaction. If the propeller is rotating clockwise, the torque reaction will tend to rotate the aircraft counter-clockwise and cause a rolling moment to the left. When on the ground, this increases the weight and friction on the left wheel, and so the aircraft yaws left.

This torque reaction also acts during flight and the aircraft feels a rolling moment opposite propeller rotation. In low-power airplanes, the reaction is small compared to the damping provided by the wings, so the aircraft only rolls slightly and the yaw is the dominant effect. However, in a high-power warbird at low airspeed (where the aerodynamic damping is least), the airplane can roll out of control if too much power is applied too quickly. A go-round from final approach is a typical case. The P-51 and similar airplanes were well known for this torque roll effect. At low airspeed, even the ailerons may not be powerful enough to stop the roll. The solution is to apply power smoothly, slowly and progressively as the airspeed increases.

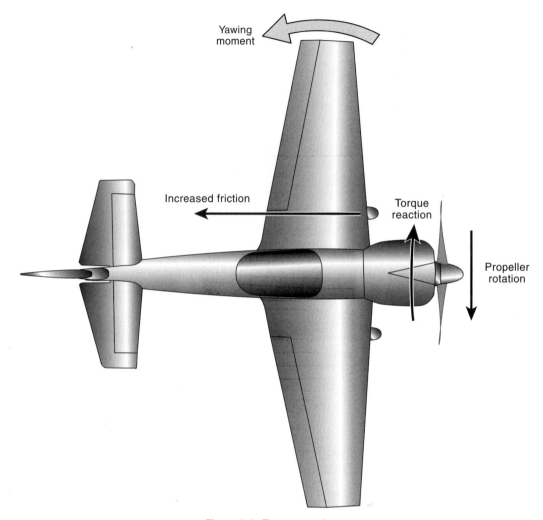

Figure 2-8. Torque reaction.

Gyroscopic Effect (Precession)

The propeller is a rotating mass and therefore has all of the properties of a gyroscope. Fortunately, most of the propeller mass is concentrated towards the hub and so this reduces the effect. If you lift a bicycle wheel on an axle and rotate it, you will feel a resistance to any change of tilt. This is caused by the rigidity of the rotating wheel that is proportional to the mass of the wheel, its mass distribution (radius) and its RPM. If you force the alignment of the axle to change, you will find that it responds out of phase; that is, if you try to roll the axle to the right and the wheel is rotating away from you, it will convert the roll input to a yaw in the same direction. This phase-change of 90° from roll to yaw and from yaw to roll is called *precession*.

Early in the takeoff run, as the tail is being raised, the airplane rotates about the main wheel axles. The nose and the propeller shaft are tilted down. The rotating mass of the propeller, as well as resisting this pitching motion, also wants to change the nose-down moment to a yaw to the left for this engine. The effect disappears as soon as the nose stops pitching.

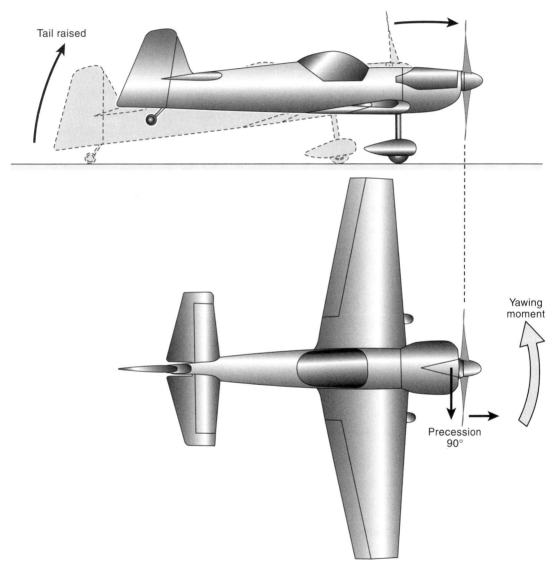

Figure 2-9. Gyroscopic effect.

Asymmetric (Non-Symmetrical) Blade Effect

When the aircraft accelerates with the tail wheel still on the ground, the propeller shaft is inclined upward and the plane of rotation of the propeller is titled rearward, but the airplane is moving horizontally. Therefore the direction of the relative airflow is different from one side of the propeller disk to the other.

The downgoing blade will have a greater angle of attack than the upcoming blade. Therefore the downgoing blade (on the right side in this case) produces more thrust and the airplane will yaw accordingly again to the left for this engine rotation.

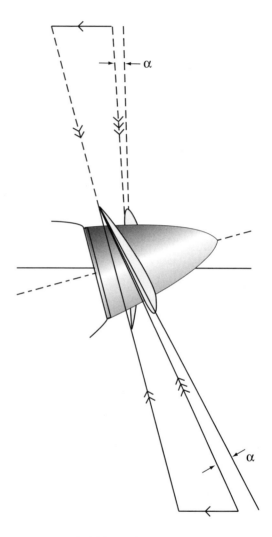

At high α, the angle of attack of downgoing blade is nearly double that of the upgoing blade ∴ nearly double the thrust

Figure 2-11. Different angles of attack.

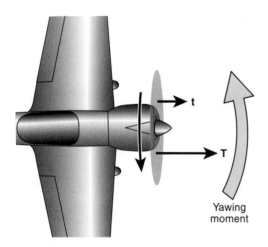

Yawing moment

Figure 2-10. Asymmetric blade effect.

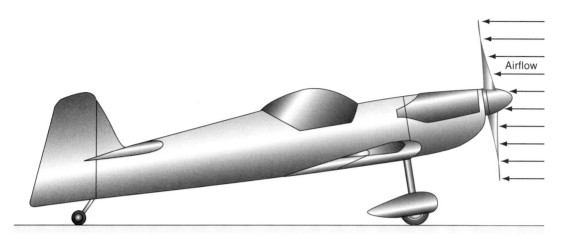

Figure 2-12. Different angle of attack due to attitude.

This effect disappears as soon as the aircraft reaches a level attitude, which is the same for the gyroscopic effect. The rudder also becomes more effective as the tail rises into the relative airflow. The directional stability increases for the same reason.

So the critical stage is during the initial process of raising the tail.

If the yawing moment is controlled at this stage, the rest becomes easier as the airplane accelerates.

Summary

Note that the above four effects cause a yaw to the left in an airplane whose propeller rotates clockwise as seen from the cockpit. This is the case for the vast majority of aircraft that use US-built engines. The pilot counters these effects with right rudder. The higher the power, and the lower the airspeed, the more rudder is required. For airplanes with counter-clockwise rotating propellers (e.g. Pratt & Whitney radial engines and the inverted Gypsy Major), the yaw on takeoff will be to the right.

There is also the need to consider the direction of any crosswind. A wind from the left, for example, will cause a swing to the left, and this could be the final straw in the control equation for an airplane with an engine that rotates to the left.

Flight Dynamics on Takeoff

Moment Change on Takeoff

Now, let's consider that the aircraft has accelerated and the pilot has raised the tail. The airplane is now accelerating in a level attitude. The pilot is working on the rudders to maintain a straight path. The rudder and elevators have a powerful moment arm because the aircraft on the ground rotates about the main wheels.

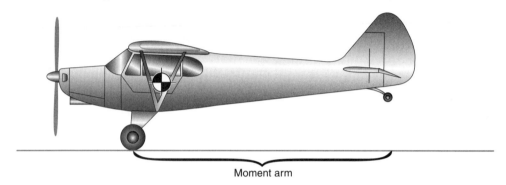

Moment arm

Figure 2-13. Rudder/elevator moment arm.

The stability and control of the aircraft are influenced by the length of the tail moment arm. As soon as the wheels leave the ground, the airplane in flight rotates about the CG, which is behind the wheels, so the moment arm is reduced. The airplane will tend to settle if back pressure was necessary to get airborne as the elevators become slightly less effective. This is not a major effect, but you will see some taildraggers skip slightly after becoming airborne. The effect is more noticeable at aft CG.

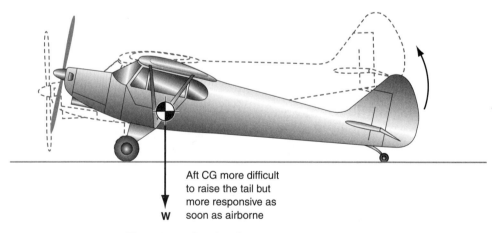

W   Aft CG more difficult to raise the tail but more responsive as soon as airborne

Figure 2-14. On takeoff, moment arm is reduced.

Dynamics and Aerodynamics in Flight

The air does not know if the airplane is a taildragger—or does it?

Adverse Aileron Yaw

The design of the antique airplane and the ultralight uses simple ailerons: they are large for low-speed effectiveness and they move equally up or down. Adverse aileron yaw is caused by the drag on the aileron deflected downward being greater than the drag on the upward aileron. This drag differential causes a yawing moment away from the direction of roll. This yaw causes a secondary rolling moment opposite the desired direction of roll, thus reducing the effect of the initial aileron deflection.

Later designs use differential ailerons, where the upward aileron travels further than the downward, thus balancing the drag. Some have Frise ailerons where the leading edge of the upward aileron protrudes into the airflow below the wing thus increasing its drag. Larger airplanes use spoilers to counter the adverse yaw.

Airplanes with these devices still may show adverse yaw with large aileron deflections at high angles of attack (low airspeed).

The imperative is that the pilot uses coordinated rudder with aileron input to counter any adverse yaw and to maximize the roll response. It is especially important on final approach and to straighten and point the nose of the aircraft in a crosswind.

Increased Rudder and Elevator Power

Since the taildragger is designed to land at the stalling angle of attack, there must be enough elevator power at minimum airspeed to still pitch the nose up. Thus the taildragger has more elevator power than the trike. Similarly, at this minimum airspeed it must have sufficient rudder to provide positive directional control. This control power is invaluable, but can cause departure from controlled flight or overstress if misused at low or high speed respectively.

Wing Drop at Stall

Because the elevator power allows the pilot to fully stall the taildragger, there is more likelihood of a wing drop at the point of stall. There is no problem if rudder is used to counter any yaw or roll. Opposite aileron is a no-no.

Flaps

Not all taildraggers have flaps so the sideslipping approach technique is invaluable for normal approaches and forced landings. Check whether your airplane is approved for sideslips, and whether there are any airspeed indicator errors under these flight conditions.

Even with flaps the sideslip is sometimes useful, but some aircraft are not approved for sideslips with the flaps extended.

Flare and Touchdown

Final Approach

On final approach, the taildragger has better control response and similar power response to tricycle airplanes. The technique for flight path and airspeed control is identical no matter the landing gear, the engine and the size of the aircraft.

Initiation of the Flare

When established on final approach, in the approach configuration and at the reference airspeed, the forces and moments acting on the airplane are balanced. The tail typically has a downward force to finally balance the pitching moments. The power of the elevators and the download on the tail is affected by the propeller slipstream (in the case of a single-engine airplane). There is also a contribution of lift from the inboard section of the wings that is enhanced by the slipstream. At high angles of attack, there is a small component of thrust that also adds to the total lifting forces.

It is important not to adjust the thrust setting between the commencement of the flare and after the flare has been initiated. If the throttle is closed before raising the nose, then there are forces and moments working against the pilot's inputs.

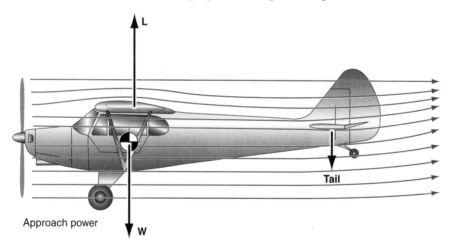

Figure 2-15. Balanced in the approach configuration.

When the throttle is closed:
- the lift is reduced;
- there is a nose-down pitching moment (remember, what happens to the nose of the airplane when you reduce power?);
- the tail cannot produce the same download;
- the elevators are less effective; and
- there is a yawing moment associated with throttle closure.

All of these factors work against the pilot in the transition from flight to ground; that is, they occur just when the workload is highest and the greatest skill and judgment are demanded.

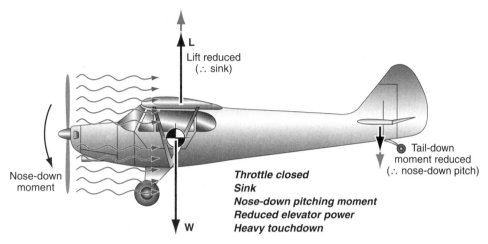

Figure 2-16. Effect of power reduction before initiating the flare.

As soon as the aircraft's flight path changes to parallel to the ground, the pilot can then slowly retard the throttle and anticipate the nose-down pitch, loss of lift and the yaw—when ready for them. The previously negative factors now actually help to discontinue the float and promote an earlier touchdown.

Flare Problems

Bounce (Under-Rotation)

If the nose is not raised sufficiently or quickly enough for the landing flare, or the throttle is closed and the nose attitude not held, then the ground contact with the main wheels will be firm and the momentum of the CG will cause an instantaneous increase in angle of attack. The aircraft will bounce from the landing gear compression and the increased lift.

Balloon (Over-Rotation)

If the nose is raised too far or too quickly or, as is commonly the case, the airspeed is higher than optimum, the aircraft will have sufficient energy to climb slightly instead of slowing to touchdown. This ballooning is a nuisance, requiring the pilot to make a second landing or, in extreme cases, to recover from a nose-high attitude with the airspeed reducing—a *hang-up*. The safest way is to go around and try again.

Recovery From a Bounce, Balloon or Hang-Up

The only safe way to regain control and contain both decaying airspeed and increasing rate of descent is with added power, sometimes enough power to go around for another approach. There is no point pulling back on the stick. The aircraft is close to stalling and the only way up or to slow the descent is by adding power.

The added power acts to hold the airspeed and cushion the touchdown. It also increases the lift and elevator control power.

Solution to Landing Flare Problems

Most difficulties with the landing flare are smoothed away if the pilot looks well ahead to the far end of the runway.

Types of Touchdown

There are two distinct ways of landing a taildragger and a third technique that is a compromise between the first two. They are:
- three-point (main and tail wheels together);
- wheeler (main wheels only); and
- tail-down wheeler (main wheels only but with the aircraft in a tail-down attitude).

Three-Point Landing

The normal landing for a taildragger is the three-point landing where all wheels touch together. The aircraft is in the prestall attitude and is at minimum flying speed. It has dissipated all excess energy and is ready to remain on the ground.

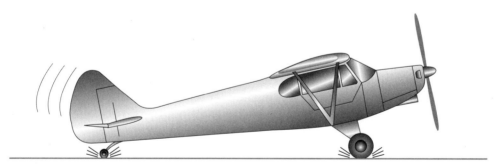

Figure 2-17. Three-point landing.

The aircraft is vulnerable to wind gusts at this high angle of attack and with the rudder shielded and the throttle closed. The pilot's view ahead may also be restricted, although the peripheral view is most effective in judging the touchdown.

Wheeler

The wheeler is made on the main wheels alone with the aircraft in a near-level attitude. On touchdown, the stick is moved forward to reduce the angle of attack and to pin the aircraft on the ground. The touchdown must be gentle and controlled. The wheeler is appropriate for some aircraft as it provides greater aerodynamic control power (to counter crosswind and gusts), a slightly higher approach speed for greater safety margin, a better forward view and a greater degree of control of the touchdown.

Figure 2-18. A wheeler.

The disadvantages are the higher threshold speed of typically 10 percent (and so a longer landing run), and the aircraft, having greater energy, is a little more lively at touchdown. It is therefore more prone to bouncing or ballooning. Being at a higher airspeed also means that a gust of wind will lift the into-wind wing, though there is more aileron power.

Tail-Down Wheeler

The compromise of a tail-down wheeler reduces the airspeed and the energy on touchdown of the wheeler, but retains a slightly better control and view than the three point landing. It is preferred by some pilots, especially in the larger taildraggers such as the DC-3.

Dynamics on Landing

Friction on Contact

As soon as the tires touch, there is friction toward the tail. The amount depends on the runway surface, the tread on the tires, and whether the brakes are applied. With this drag comes a nose-down pitching moment, but this is easily overcome by back stick.

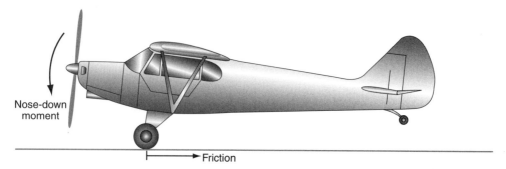

Figure 2-19. Wheel friction causes momentary nose-down pitch.

Bounce

A firm arrival has the reverse effect to the friction on contact since the downward momentum of the CG causes an increase in the angle of attack and a bounce back into the air.

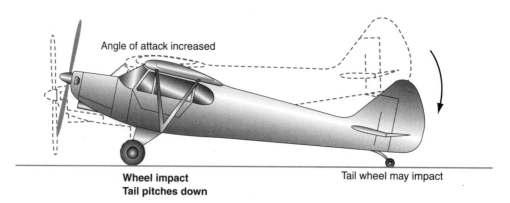

Figure 2-20. Mechanics of a bounce.

Tail Moment Arm

With the change from flight to ground, there is also a change of tail moment arm, so the elevators have less effect and, unless the tail wheel is on the ground, the tail will tend to drop. This causes an increase in angle of attack and, unless the speed is correct, any excess energy will result in a bounce (lift back into the air).

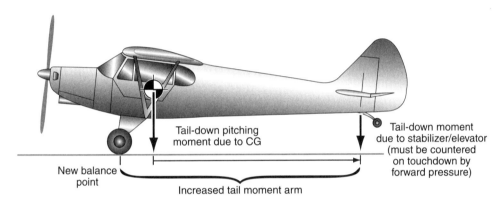

Figure 2-21. Wheeler landing touchdown.

Yaw/Swing/Ground Loop

On landing, the same dynamics apply as for takeoff. However, the pilot's control is reduced due to the lack of propeller slipstream, and because the fin and rudder are buried in the wake of disturbed air behind the fuselage. The pilot has to be actively diligent to prevent the build up of any yaw and to ensure there is no drift on touchdown, which can result in yaw.

If the landing was not on three points, there is a further danger area. The point from tail-level touchdown, when the tail begins to drop, to tail wheel contact is critical for several reasons:

• there is a gyroscopic moment due to the changing angle of attack of the propeller; and
• the fin and rudder drop into the wash from the fuselage and so lose their dynamic airflow, thus becoming less effective.

Aerodynamics on Landing

Ground Effect

As the airplane gets closer to the ground, there is a reaction of the pressured air under the wing against the ungiving surface of the runway. This reaction adds to the lift reaction and so tends to cushion the arrival. In the same way, a helicopter hovering near the ground is able to lift more.

For the same total lift, there is also a reduced angle of attack and therefore reduced induced drag. Hence, the extended float that you see by some landing aircraft, especially if their speed is a little high.

Typically, ground effect increases the closer the wing is to the ground. Above a smooth surface, especially water, it starts at a height equivalent to half the aircraft's wingspan. A long-winged airplane has significant ground effect at a reasonable height.

Have you read about bombers in World War II losing an engine or two, only able to maintain altitude when within a few feet of the water? They could then fly all the way home as not only was the lift now better, but the reduced drag allowed the aircraft to maintain speed and to reach home on the remaining fuel.

Ground effect is less noticeable over uneven terrain.

A high-wing airplane has less pronounced ground effect as, for the same aircraft height, the wing is further from the ground. Conversely, a low wing has a more pronounced effect because the wing surface is closer to the ground.

Span, Aspect Ratio and Sweep

Aspect ratio is the ratio of span to average chord, or span squared over wing area. Thus, for the same total area, a wing with a high aspect ratio has greater span and so greater ground effect. A sailplane glides a long way in ground effect. A low wing airplane has a more noticeable ground effect because the wing is closer to the ground.

Adverse Aileron Yaw

With the control in the flare, there is an inevitable interaction between yaw and roll, and vice versa. In the flare before touchdown, this relationship becomes important. As the pilot yaws the airplane straight, it will want to roll in the direction of the yaw. Thus the pilot needs to apply opposite aileron.

If the aircraft is sideslipping (wing down), it will want to roll opposite to the direction of sideslip. Aircraft with sweepback and higher aspect ratio have more pronounced roll due to yaw and roll due to sideslip.

When yawing straight from a crabbed approach, the roll due to yaw is significant. Get to know your aircraft and how much opposite aileron is needed.

You also should over-roll a little, lowering the into-wind wing to prevent drift from building up before touchdown.

Part Two

Flight Techniques

Chapter 3

Ground Operations

Safe operation of the taildragger on the ground encompasses:
- preflight and prestart actions;
- engine starting;
- taxiing;
- run-up and pretakeoff checks; and
- shutdown and security procedures.

Preflight and Prestart

Airframe Inspection

As well as the daily maintenance checks by technical staff, there is always a need for the aircraft to be inspected before and after each flight. There may be one standard inspection, or one major daily inspection before the first flight of the day with an abbreviated inspection between flights. Check with your instructor. A close inspection is especially important for the taildragger.

Always drain some fuel to check for water and contaminants every day and after every refuelling or, better still, before every flight.

Common preflight items are:
- Untie and unlock the aircraft.
- Ideally, lift the tail and pivot the aircraft so it points into the wind (especially an ultralight). Have a wingwalker to assist and hold the wing down as you do so. A wingwalker is handy when taxiing also.
- Remove all covers and blanks.
- Remove the control locks provided the wind will not force the control surfaces to severe deflections. If there is any significant wind, check the controls and then tie the control column back.
- Check the seat-back, rails and locks. Many taildraggers have been lost due to seat-back, track or lock failure on takeoff. It is more important than a trike as the seat and seat-back tend to be overstressed and fatigued because they are used as a handrail, lever and physical support when entering or leaving the cockpit.
- Apply the parking brake, check the ignition switches are off and turn on the master switch and external lights.

- Remove the chocks (unless you have someone to remove them after start) and check the stall warning device and the lights.
- Return to the cockpit, note the fuel gauge readings and turn off the lights and master switch.
- Complete an external inspection especially focusing on the flight controls (full deflection and unrestricted movement), flap operation, fuel and oil contents, hydraulic fluid leaks around the brakes, hydraulic hoses on landing gear legs, tires for inflation and wear. A soft tire will considerably lengthen the takeoff run and will affect directional control—the soft tire will drag and sink. We have enough challenges with a taildragger without these added complexities.
- In particular, check the main gear struts for compression. There is a tell-tale mark or use the width of your fingers as a guide (e.g. four fingers for the gear leg, two for a glass of scotch). Check the tail wheel assembly for corrosion, cracks and damage to the leg, pivot, centering springs and cables. Remove any grass or mud from the assembly. Check the tire is not cracked nor split. If the tire is part of the rudder assembly, as it is on some homebuilts, check it is free to move in its housing and not choked with grass or mud.
- Look for stone damage and evidence of a heavy landing or ground loop—scratches, scrapes and dents on the airframe, especially underneath and on the flaps and empennage.
- Check the propeller carefully for nicks, cuts and cracks (have them filed professionally to remove stress concentrations).
- Look for signs of straw, grass, bugs or nests in the engine cowling, especially the radiator for liquid-cooled engines and the oil cooler.

Always carry a cloth to clean smears and spills so that, after the flight, you can see whether there are fresh leaks.

Check the cleanliness of the windscreen and windows and clean only with a wet chamois (*shammy*) cloth and approved cleaner. Do not use any other cloth or paper towel, nor any soap, detergent, abrasive or household cleaning agent. Ask your technician how to correctly clean an acrylic windscreen.

Prior to starting the engine, check that the surrounding area is suitable for start-up. The airplane should be on a surface suitable for taxiing and well away from any buildings, fuel storage areas and public areas. The airplane should be parked facing in a direction that will not cause loose stones or gravel to be blasted back over other aircraft or into open hangars when the engine is running. Preferably it should be pointed into the wind.

There should also be no fuel spills in the vicinity and none under the aircraft, especially near the engine exhausts.

The aircraft and engine then needs to be prepared for the start-up. The correct procedure for this is found in your pilot's operating handbook or checklist.

Engine Start

Make sure the parking brake is applied or keep the chocks in place. Check the area is clear of people and shout *starting engine!* or *stand clear of the propeller!*

There is a risk of the aircraft pitching forward on start, especially if you have a hot start with the throttle open. Hold the stick back firmly during start (use your thighs).

Place your hand on the mixture lever after the starter is engaged in case you have to shut down quickly. Check the oil pressure rises within 30 seconds.

Taxiing

Moving Forward

Before commencing to taxi, plan the path that you will follow, taking note of the surface and the position of other aircraft. Ensure that tie-down ropes and chocks have been removed before releasing the parking brake (likewise the pitot cover!).

As soon as the aircraft starts to roll, retard the throttle and check the brakes. If there is any softening of the resistance in the pedals, then do not taxi. Stop and shut down the engine.

Maintain a normal walking pace, and avoid using power against brake (unless a high idling speed is required for better engine cooling). Cross ridges and small ditches at an angle, avoiding long grass and rough ground, and have an escape route in mind in case of brake failure. Hold the control column to prevent wind gusts from deflecting the control surfaces, and always hold the control column rearwards to maintain downward pressure on the tail wheel to improve steering and to stop the tail lifting over bumps. When crossing bumps or soft surfaces, be very aware of the propeller clearance.

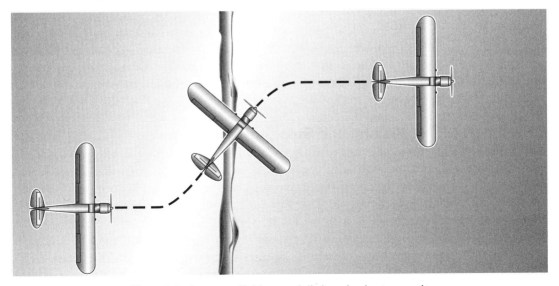

Figure 3-1. Cross small ridges and ditches slowly at an angle.

Taxiing Speed

Power is used to commence taxiing an airplane. The effects of wheel friction and the brakes are used to stop it. Like all objects, an airplane has inertia and is resistant to change, so it requires more power to start moving than to keep moving. Once the airplane is rolling at taxiing speed, the power can simply be reduced to balance the frictional forces and any air resistance so that a steady speed is maintained. On a straight and smooth taxiway with no obstructions, a fast walking pace is a safe taxiing speed, and this can be judged by looking ahead and to the left of the airplane. In a confined area, the ideal speed is somewhat less.

The amount of power required to maintain taxiing speed depends on the ground surface and its slope—a rough, upward-sloping grassy surface requiring much more power than a flat, sealed taxiway. High power may also be required to turn the airplane, especially at low speeds.

To slow the airplane down, the power should be reduced. Friction may cause the airplane to decelerate sufficiently, otherwise the brakes can be used gently, but firmly. Generally speaking, power should not be used against brakes; that is, if you wish to slow down, first close the throttle. It is a waste of energy to have excess power and be slowing the aircraft with braking. It will lead to overheated brakes, as well as increased brake wear, both of which decrease the effectiveness of the brakes should you need maximum braking to abort a takeoff.

Some aircraft have engines with a high idle RPM, and occasional braking may be required to avoid excessive taxi speed.

Also, some aircraft have a castering tail wheel and therefore the aircraft is steered by brakes. In this instance, it is almost inevitable to have some power applied while trying to brake and steer.

Initially, there is a natural tendency to steer with the control column and, of course, nothing happens. At first, taxi for a while with your hands on your lap. It is normal to hold the control column while taxiing, though, to protect the control surfaces from being damaged by wind gusts or to prevent the wind lifting the tail or wing.

Braking and Steering Technique

Brake cylinders are situated on top of each rudder pedal. They are individually applied using the ball of each foot. Normally, taxi with your heels on the floor and the balls of your feet on the rudder pedals, thereby avoiding inadvertent application of the toe brakes. When braking is needed, slide your feet up and, with the ball of each foot, apply the toe brakes as required.

To brake the airplane while taxiing in a straight line, both brakes should be applied evenly, but you may have to steer with the rudder pedals at the same time. There is a tendency to freeze the rudder movement while applying the brakes. It is simply a matter of practice.

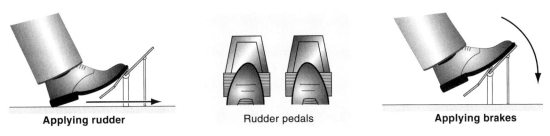

Applying rudder   **Rudder pedals**   **Applying brakes**

Figure 3-2. Using rudder and using toe brakes.

Some antiques are fitted with heel brakes separate from the rudder pedals.

Brakes should be used gently so that the airplane responds smoothly, harsh braking being avoided except in an emergency. For a normal stop, a good technique is to relax the braking pressure (or perhaps even release it) just as the airplane comes to a halt. The resulting stop will be smooth. Differential braking is available by pressing each toe brake individually. This is useful both for turning sharply and for maintaining directional control when taxiing in a strong crosswind (after applying rudder or tail wheel steering).

During extended taxiing, the brakes should be tested occasionally, and they should certainly be tested just prior to entering a congested tarmac area. Always have an escape route in mind to avoid collisions in case the brakes fail to stop the airplane.

Allow for the fact that the wings of an airplane are wide and the tail section is well behind the main wheels. Maintain a good lookout ahead and to the sides. If the taxi path is obscured by the nose, then turning slightly left and right will permit a better view. Should you unfortunately run into anything while taxiing, stop the airplane, shut down the engine, set the brakes to park, turn the master switch off and investigate.

Brake Failure

If the brakes fail:
- close the throttle; and
- steer away from other aircraft and obstacles and towards a high-friction surface if possible (e.g. grass).

If a collision is imminent:
- pull the mixture control to idle cut-off (to stop the engine);
- turn the ignition switches off;
- turn the master switch off; and
- switch the fuel off.

Ground Surface Condition

Ensure that propeller clearance will be adequate when taxiing in long grass or over rough ground, especially if there are small ditches or holes. Striking long grass or the ground can seriously damage the propeller and the engine.

Loose stones or gravel picked up and blown back in the slipstream can also damage both the propeller and the airframe. Damage may even be caused to other airplanes or persons quite some distance behind. So when taxiing on loose surfaces, avoid the use of high power as much as possible. Small ridges or ditches should be crossed at an angle so that the wheels pass across the obstruction one at a time. This will minimize stress on the landing gear and avoid the nose pitching up and down excessively, which puts the propeller at risk.

However, be careful not to straddle a hump and risk a propeller strike. Hold the control column fully rearward, and the propeller slipstream will maximize propeller clearance and help the aircraft negotiate humps and bumps. This also applies to patches of wet or soft ground. Whenever you need to increase power to keep moving, pull back on the control column. Large ditches or ridges should be avoided altogether. It is no disgrace to park the airplane, shut down the engine and walk the ground before proceeding.

Wind Effect

The flight controls should be held in a position to avoid either the tail or a wing being lifted by a strong wind.

Head Wind. When taxiing into a strong head wind, hold the control column either neutral or back. This holds the elevator neutral or up, and the tail down.

Tail Wind. When taxiing with a strong tail wind (stronger than the propeller slipstream), hold the control column forward to move the elevator down. This stops the wind lifting the horizontal stabilizer from behind.

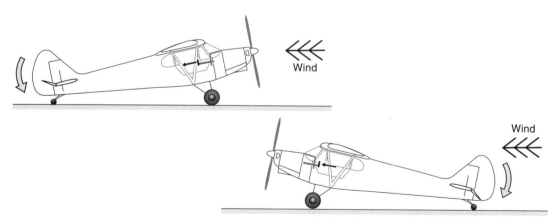

Figure 3-3. Taxi into-wind with the control column neutral or back, and taxi downwind with the control column forward.

Crosswind. A crosswind will try to weathercock the airplane into the wind because of the large keel surfaces behind the main wheels. The rudder and tail wheel should provide adequate directional control but, if not, then use differential braking. To avoid a crosswind lifting the into-wind wing, raise its aileron by moving the control column into the wind.

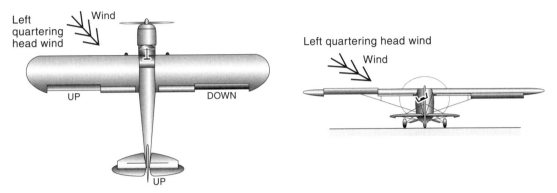

Figure 3-4. Taxiing with a left quartering head wind.

To avoid a crosswind from behind lifting the into-wind wing, lower its aileron so that the wind cannot get under it, by moving the control column out of wind.

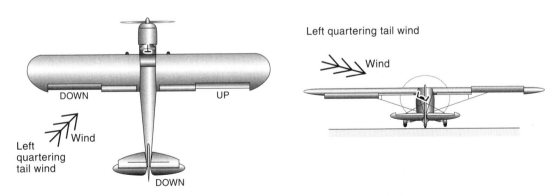

Figure 3-5. Taxiing with a left quartering tail wind.

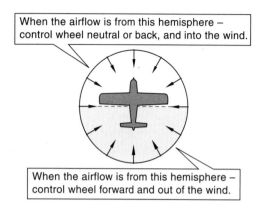

When the airflow is from this hemisphere – control wheel neutral or back, and into the wind.

When the airflow is from this hemisphere – control wheel forward and out of the wind.

Figure 3-6. Summary of the use of controls when taxiing in windy conditions.

The rotorwash, propwash or jet blast of another airplane or helicopter will produce the same effect as a wind, so always be cautious if you have to taxi close to other aircraft. Avoid taxiing behind an aircraft during its engine run-up, especially at an angle, where the propwash could lift one wing or the tail.

Checks

Run-Up Checks and Pretakeoff Vital Actions

The checks are completed in the run-up bay or some area clear of the runway. Park the aircraft pointing into wind if possible. It reduces the stress on the propeller and shaft during run-up and gives a more accurate indication of engine performance.

Make sure the brakes are parked but keep a look outside just in case. Keep the stick back at all times especially before increasing power. Check there is no other aircraft behind you before you increase power.

The vital actions are called vital because they sustain life. They are that important. The manufacturer will specify the checks for your aircraft but at least include:

T Throttle friction—Adjusted
　　Trim—Set for takeoff

M 　　Mixture—Full rich and carburetor heat to cold

P 　　Propeller—Full fine
　　Primer—Locked

F 　　Fuel—Tank selected, contents okay, boost pump on
　　Flaps—Up (or takeoff)

I 　Instruments—Checked altimeter set, compass aligned

S 　　Switches—Both

C 　　Controls—Full and free movement

H 　　Hatches—Closed and locked
　　Harnesses—Secure, seats firmly locked

As you taxi to the holding point check the wind direction and strength and make mental allowances for the effect that it will have. Look for signs of wind at pattern altitude to assess the gradient. Look for trees and other structures that may induce turbulence in the takeoff roll and immediately after liftoff. Do not turn downwind after takeoff until at normal climb speed, clear of terrain and positively climbing.

Postflight and Security Actions

Engine Shutdown

There will be a shutdown procedure specified in the pilot's operating handbook for your aircraft which will include such items as:

- Parking brakes applied, with the airplane (ideally) pointing into any strong wind.
- Ensure the engine is cool (having taxied or setting 1,000 to 1,200 RPM for a minute should be sufficient).
- Both magnetos should be checked individually. There should be a slight RPM drop as you go from both to an individual magneto, and a return to the set RPM when the switch is returned to both.

Note that sometimes a *dead-cut check* is made by moving the ignition switch very quickly from *both* to *off* and back to *both* to check that the engine will actually cut. This checks that the off position does indeed break the circuit to each magneto by grounding them. If this were not the case, the engine and propeller would be live even with the magneto switched off. In such a case, an innocent movement of the propeller could start the engine unexpectedly—a dangerous situation! Some engine manufacturers advise against this check as it may damage the engine, especially if the switch is held too long in the off position. Seek your instructor's advice. Then:

- all individual electrical services off (radio, lights, etc.);
- avionics master off;
- mixture control set to idle cut-off (fully out) to starve the engine of fuel and stop it running;
- after the engine stops, switch the ignition off and remove the key; and
- alternator and battery master switch off.

Postflight Inspection

An airplane has a life of its own in the sense that it passes continually from the command of one pilot to the command of another, the postflight check of one being followed by the preflight check of the next. To a certain extent, each pilot relies on the fact that previous pilots have performed their duties, even though we must all accept individual responsibility. After your flight, check for leaks (they will be obvious if you cleaned the aircraft during the preflight), general wear and tear, possible stone or bird strike damage and tail scrapes. Check the landing gear, brakes and tires, especially the tail wheel assembly. Check the propeller.

Securing the Airplane

The airplane should not be left unattended unless it is adequately secured against movement and possible damage. Then:
- ensure that the parking brake is on (if required) and that the wheel chocks are in place, in front of and behind the wheels;
- fit the pitot covers;
- secure the seat belts;
- if yours is the last flight of the day, consider refuelling to minimize overnight condensation of water in the fuel tanks;
- double-check all switches are off;
- lock the door and return the key; and
- complete the paperwork, the postflight documentation.

Tie-Down

At the end of a flight, consideration should be given to the safety of the airplane if it is to be left outside overnight or if strong winds or a weather change is forecast. A taildragger sits at an angle of high lift. Wind gusts can lift and overturn the airplane more readily than a tricycle, which sits in a level attitude. Park the airplane into wind or facing into any expected wind, set the brakes to park (refer to the flight manual to check if this is recommended for your airplane) and chock the wheels. Chock both in front of and behind the wheels to prevent movement in any direction.

Lock the controls/control surfaces. Some aircraft have an internal control column lock, which may consist of a pin that locks the tube from the control column and may even obscure the ignition and start switches (to prevent the pilot starting and taking off with the controls locked). Other aircraft have external metal or wooden locks that can be fitted in the gap between the control surface and fixed structure, to prevent control surface movement. It may be necessary to use the seat belt to restrain the control column (stick or wheel) to prevent damage. It is vital to prevent the control surfaces being forced to maximum deflection in windy conditions. Violent deflections in reverse airflow damage the hinges, cables, bellcranks and pushrods.

Tie down the aircraft. There are tie-down rings designed into the airplane structure, under the wings and at the tail. On a grass field, you may have to drive pegs into the ground and attach the tie-down ropes to them. The ropes attached to the wing should be angled forward and out. Check the correct procedure for your aircraft and school.

The tail tie-down is vital for the taildragger. For extreme forecast winds, position the airplane in the lee of a building, trees or hangar, face into the wind, perhaps raise the tail onto a support and tie down in a near-level attitude. Secure the control surfaces.

Chapter 4

Normal Takeoff

The takeoff maneuver involves:
- preparing for takeoff and configuring the aircraft;
- accelerating to flying speed as quickly as possible (tail up) while maintaining directional control;
- flying the airplane off the ground and clearing any obstacles;
- establishing the initial climb attitude and flight path while the aircraft is reconfigured (landing gear, flaps, power and boost pump);
- entering a normal climb (best rate of climb) with a turn to crosswind or the outbound track; and
- leveling and positioning the airplane for departure or the crosswind/downwind leg.

Takeoff Performance

Factors Affecting Takeoff Performance
Consider:
- takeoff direction;
- runway length;
- runway slope;
- runway surface;
- density altitude;
- wind velocity;
- wind gradient;
- turbulence;
- aircraft configuration;
- takeoff weight and CG position;
- aircraft condition, especially engine and propeller; and
- pilot familiarity with the field, the aircraft type and the conditions.

Takeoff Direction
Normal takeoff for a taildragger is made as closely as possible into the wind for the following reasons:
- shortest ground run;
- lowest ground speed on liftoff;

- best directional control, at the start of the ground run, when there is little airflow over the control surfaces;
- no side forces on the landing gear (as in a crosswind);
- best obstacle clearance due to the shorter ground run and the steeper climb path; and
- best position from which to make an into-wind landing in the case of engine failure immediately after takeoff.

If not into wind, it is best to choose a takeoff direction in which the crosswind counters the dynamic and slipstream effects; that is, for most aircraft, take off with the crosswind from the right so the yaw due to the wind opposes the yaw due to other effects.

Effects of Wind

Constant Wind Velocity

A steady wind is actually better than no wind provided it is mostly down the runway. However, with any wind there will be a change with height above ground. Therefore, with a head wind at ground level, it will be stronger and perhaps have a different direction away from the ground. Typically, the wind will increase in speed away from the ground; for takeoff into wind, the aircraft is climbing into an increasing head wind, which steepens the climb and tends to increase the airspeed—all good news.

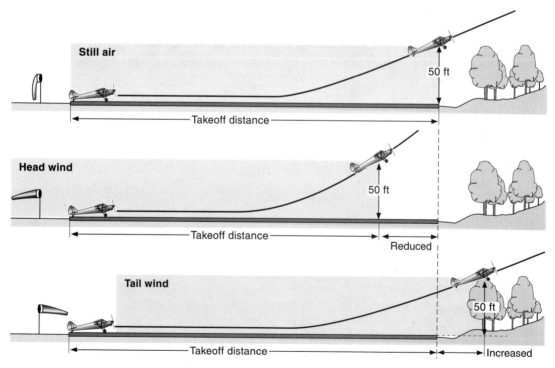

Figure 4-1. Effect of wind on takeoff.

Wind Gradients

Taking off downwind, as well as lengthening the takeoff roll, risks climbing into an increasing tail wind: the effect is a little like trying to catch a bus that is accelerating away from you! The wind shear tends to decrease your airspeed, hence the nose must be lowered to retain the desired indicated airspeed. This and the increased movement over the ground cause the climb angle to be degraded. If you are climbing at V_X there is little airspeed margin above the stall.

Another situation to avoid is turning after takeoff. If there is a significant crosswind and you turn away from the wind, you risk a momentary loss of airspeed, an increasing ground speed and a reduced climb gradient. It is better to turn into a crosswind after takeoff, if you can.

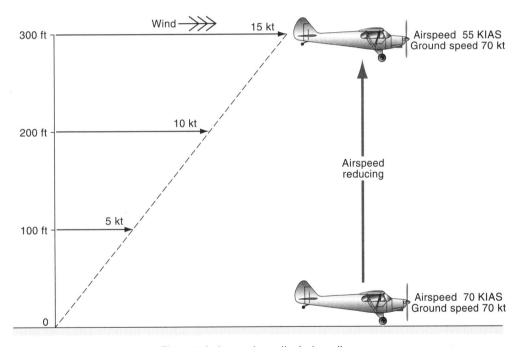

Figure 4-2. Increasing tail wind gradient.

Wind Shear

Shear refers to a noticeable rather than a subtle change of wind with changing levels. There is a momentary airspeed fluctuation, perhaps serious at obstacle climb speed. When experiencing wind shear, you can only leave full power set and adjust the attitude to restore the desired airspeed and flight path, but do not *chase* the airspeed fluctuations.

Wind Gusts

A gusting wind is bad news for the taildragger as it requires even more positive control activity by the pilot. It can be hard work. Always respect the demonstrated maximum crosswind recommended by the aircraft's manufacturer and apply the limit to gusts; for example, if the demonstrated limit is 15 knots and the wind is 10 knots gusting to 20 knots, don't go.

Thermals

Hot summer conditions produce vertical air movement as well as horizontal. This mixing can also cause spiral motions called *dust devils* or, in Australia, *willy-willies*. They are generally visible by the dust they stir up. Stay clear of them as they can pick up one wing. They are generally of a small diameter and short-lived. Wait a few minutes until it passes clear.

Turbulence

Turbulence suggests some downdrafts and some disruption to accurate flying; both of which reduce the aircraft's best climb angle and climb rate.

Runway Considerations

Length

The takeoff performance chart should be consulted if you are not certain that the runway is adequate in all respects. High-elevation airfields and high temperatures will increase the runway distances required due to the decreased air density that degrades both engine and aerodynamic performance. Runway upslope and a tail wind component will also degrade the takeoff.

Surface

Any element that increases friction on the wheels is adverse to takeoff performance. Water, long grass, mud, dust, potholes and uneven ground all extend the takeoff ground run.

Slope

Runway slope is very significant. If it is more than a couple of degrees, then it may be better to takeoff the other way even with a slight tail wind. Discuss the performance of your aircraft with your instructor.

Aircraft Condition and Configuration

Flaps

Some aircraft use a small amount of flap deflection for takeoff if it gives greater value in terms of lift than penalty due to increased drag. Your aircraft will have a specified configuration for normal takeoffs. Use of takeoff flaps may shorten the takeoff run. Extending takeoff flaps increases the lifting ability of the wings, enabling the airplane to take off at a lower airspeed and with a shorter ground run. It is more appropriate for use on a shorter runway when it is important to lift off at the lowest possible speed.

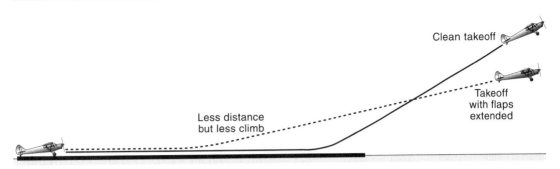

Figure 4-3. Flaps allow a shorter takeoff ground run.

Landing flaps are never used for takeoff because the significant increase in drag will degrade the takeoff and climb-out performance. It is an important check for a stop-and-go landing that the landing flap is retracted. For a touch-and-go, follow your aircraft's procedures. Some aircraft behave better if the flaps are left until after the takeoff; others require the flaps to be reset during the ground roll. Moreover, be careful not to exceed the recommended flap settings for takeoff nor the flap limiting speed after takeoff.

Takeoff Weight and CG Position

Acceleration depends on the amount of thrust the engine can supply and the weight of the aircraft. The greater the weight, the less the acceleration, and therefore the greater the takeoff distance. Increased weight means increased wheel friction. Increased weight also requires an increased liftoff speed, again requiring greater runway distance.

A forward CG position reduces the power of the elevators and, therefore, increases the force the pilot must apply to lift off. An aft CG position makes it easier. As long as the aircraft is loaded within prescribed limits, there is no problem.

Aircraft Condition

An older aircraft will inevitably have some engine and propeller wear; therefore it will not produce quite as much thrust as a new one. Propeller nicks, though filed out, still affect the shape and the aerodynamic efficiency of the propeller. The performance charts assume an aircraft in peak condition.

Anything that adversely affects the aerodynamic shape of the wing or adds to the weight of the aircraft will have a similarly adverse effect on takeoff performance. The acceleration will be slower, liftoff speed will be higher, and therefore ground roll and initial climb will be extended.

Any foreign matter attached to the wing such as mud and ice will not only spoil the shape of the wing, but will add to the weight—both adverse factors. Always clean the aircraft of substantial mud or ice. Washing the aircraft will remove both but, on a very cold day, the water can refreeze before you are ready to takeoff.

Density Altitude

Engine performance reduces with thinner air. This occurs at higher airfield elevations, high surface temperatures and high humidity. The less dense air means the aircraft has to reach a higher ground speed to generate the same lift as in air that is more dense. The effects are very significant and should be checked in your aircraft's performance charts.

Pilot Technique

The aircraft takeoff distance and climb performance assumes a correct takeoff technique. Incorrect flap or propeller setting, slow power application (more than two or three seconds), early or late rotation to a takeoff attitude or holding the aircraft to a shallow initial climb all affect the planned takeoff distance and obstacle clearance.

Takeoff Flight Technique

Lineup

It is important to check the windsock just before you release the brakes. (I make it a habit to double-check the windsock and the flight controls before I apply power on every takeoff.) Line up, hold the control column firmly back, ensure that the tail wheel is straight (that it clicks into the detent) and have the aircraft moving straight. If the tailwheel has a mechanical lock then engage it now. Check the compass and heading indicator. Unless the runway length is marginal keep the aircraft rolling and smoothly apply full power (about three seconds to reach full throttle).

Place your heels on the floor with the balls of your feet on the rudder pedals to control steering (but not high enough to inadvertently apply the brakes). Apply rudder by sliding your heel forward rather than by depressing the pedal.

Takeoff Roll

Select a reference point at the center of the far end of the runway by which to keep straight (figure 4-4).

In side-by-side cockpits, you should view this reference point straight ahead (parallel with the longitudinal axis of the airplane), not over the propeller spinner. Some cowls have a convenient join or hinge line; otherwise, I would paint a narrow reference line on the cowl or use a short strip of narrow tape (figure 4-5).

Glance at the tachometer early in the takeoff run to confirm that maximum RPM has been set and check that the airspeed is increasing. You will get to know the acceleration for your airplane. If it does not feel right, close the throttle and abort the takeoff.

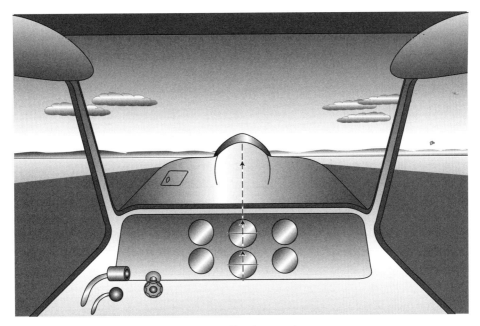

Figure 4-4. Tandem seating.

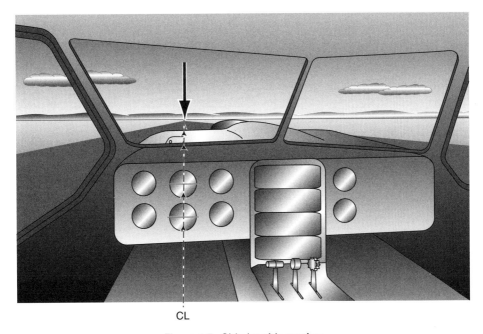

CL

Figure 4-5. Side-by-side seating.

Keep Straight with Rudder

With the application of power, there will be a tendency to yaw because of the:
- slipstream effect on the fin;
- asymmetric blade effect; and
- torque reaction pressing one wheel down.

In no wind, an airplane whose propeller rotates clockwise, as seen from the cockpit, will yaw left on takeoff. If the propeller rotates counterclockwise, it will yaw right.

Use your reference point to stop any yaw before it starts. Large and quick rudder applications may be required early in the takeoff run. Allow the aircraft to run forward and build a little speed before applying positive forward stick to raise the tail (some aircraft require full forward control). As the airflow over the rudder increases, and the tail is lifted out of the wake of the fuselage, smaller movements will be sufficient. Be ready for the swing as the tail comes up. Just look ahead and keep the airplane tracking straight down the centerline.

Apply aileron into any known crosswind.

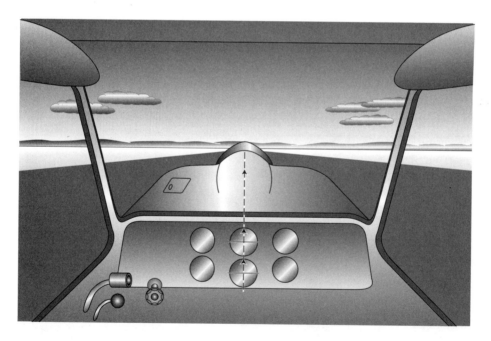

Figure 4-6. Raising the tail.

Expect the swing as the tail comes up due to gyroscopic effect and in the same direction as the torque reaction (figures 4-7 and 4-8).

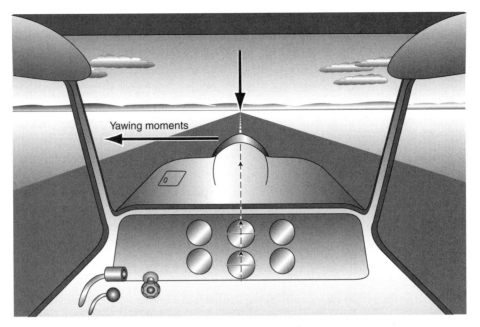

Figure 4-7. Airplane will yaw as tail comes up.

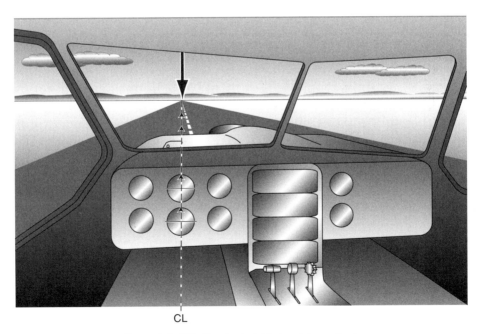

Figure 4-8. Liftoff attitude (side-by-side seating).

Liftoff

When the level attitude is reached, maintain it (do not overdo it and reduce the propeller clearance). Continue to keep straight and continue to look at the far end of the runway. It is the best reference to use to keep straight and to hold a correct level attitude. The dynamic forces, tending to yaw the aircraft (other than the wind) will now have dissipated and the slipstream effect reduces with forward speed.

The aircraft will come alive as the weight shifts to the wings and it starts to lift from the wheels. When it feels ready, lift off positively and hold that liftoff attitude while the aircraft accelerates to initial climb speed. Do not look inside at this stage. Keep the wings level and allow the aircraft to yaw if it wants to.

If you lift off before the aircraft is ready, the airplane will not fly. It will skip and will settle back onto the ground. Control of both pitch and yaw is difficult in these circumstances, acceleration is retarded and the airplane consumes more runway. Conversely, do not force the aircraft to stay on the ground when it is buoyant and ready to fly: the wheels and tires will be subjected to extra stress, directional control will be difficult and the takeoff will be unnecessarily prolonged. You also reduce the propeller clearance and risk a prop-strike. To avoid this, look well ahead of the nose. Looking too close as the tail comes up causes the pilot to point the nose lower. Holding that low nose attitude keeps the airplane on the ground for too long.

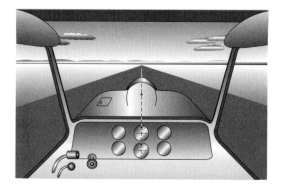 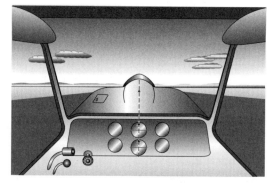

Figure 4-9. Gradually assume the climb attitude.

Ground effect allows takeoff at lower speeds and there is less induced drag than when the airplane is well clear of the ground. It is important that the airplane is accelerating and is close to the optimum climbing speed before it leaves ground effect; otherwise, the aircraft may slow and sink for a moment. Similarly, flap retraction should be delayed until normal climb speed and safe terrain clearance is guaranteed, generally more than 200 feet above the ground.

Initial Climb and Turn

After takeoff, a straight climb is made to at least 500 feet above airfield elevation. During this initial climb, there is a delicate balance between climbing and accelerating related to, at the same time, retracting the landing gear and flaps, adjusting the power, turning off the boost pump and retrimming. Get to know where things are in your cockpit. You should be able to place your hand on each control without looking inside. (Chuck Yeager sat in the cockpit of his rocket plane, in the dark, until he could confidently find every switch and lever. If it's good enough for Chuck...)

The important aspect for us is to maintain the visual attitude immediately after liftoff, and especially to keep the wings level.

Energy, Momentum, Wind

Altitude is safety. It is vital that the first turn is done above 500 feet AGL. Turning reduces climb performance. The initial climb and turn are also affected by wind, turbulence and downdrafts. Take into account any high terrain after takeoff and on the departure track.

Avoid turning downwind in the initial climb if there is a terrain problem. Turning downwind not only reduces the climb gradient but reduces airspeed and compounds the problem. A turn into a head wind increases airspeed and steepens the climb angle. Try to avoid passing on the lee (downwind) side of a hill or large obstacle to avoid downdrafts.

Low-Inertia Airplanes

The period immediately after liftoff, and before the climb is well established at 500 feet AGL or more, is a critical time for engine failure in any airplane, but especially so for a low-inertia airplane. Many of the antique airplanes and ultralights have low momentum and high drag. Many will not pitch nose-down with engine failure quickly enough to maintain flying speed unless the pilot makes a positive control input.

In the initial climb, pay attention to nothing but climbing straight ahead and being ready for possible engine failure. Do not relax, do not reduce power, and do not turn until above 500 feet AGL. Be careful selecting flaps up if they were used for takeoff. Bring them up slowly, in stages, at normal climb speed and not below 200 feet AGL.

Regularly practice climb-attitude engine failures at a safe altitude. Get to know the control input required for your airplane at maximum weight and rearward CG. If the engine does quit, choose a field ahead, lower flaps and land. Do not turn unless you have altitude to spare.

A Takeoff in Practice

Let's consider the mind of an experienced aviator thinking aloud during a takeoff:

Approaching the holding point for Runway 18. I'll check the windsock once more.

Good. The surface wind is almost down the runway: a little from the left (about 150° at 10 knots) so the swing on takeoff will be a little more pronounced than usual. No problem.

The runway is in good shape and plenty long enough. The surface is firm and dry and the slope is insignificant. There are some trees on the left side so there could be a little sink.

The forecast is for a wind at 2,000 feet of 220/20 so there's a gradient and I can expect to lose a little airspeed as I turn left. I'll take off normally but allow the aircraft to accelerate 10 knots above maximum angle-of-climb speed before setting climb attitude and power. This will give a little insurance against airspeed decay. (I'll pick up a little speed initially, but it will decay as I climb.)

There may be some turbulence and sink in the lee of the hills to the south-east. I'll stay well clear.

OK. Controls free, lined up, tail wheel straight, looking at the far end of the runway, full power, feet off the brakes. Holding the stick back until there is forward speed. Left aileron to stop the wing lifting. Now forward stick to raise the tail, together with more right rudder pressure. Anticipate the left swing. Hold the level attitude—acceleration is good—I am go.

Holding aileron into wind. Lifting. Weight coming off the wheels. Back pressure, clean liftoff, allowing the plane to weathercock into wind. Keep the wings level. Hold that attitude and allow the plane to accelerate in ground effect until $V_X + 10$. Now slowly increase attitude to normal climb speed + 10. Engine failure now and I'll put the plane back down on the runway.

Positive rate of climb, no runway remaining (gear up), hold that attitude. There's a clear field to the left if I need it; watch out for the power lines, though. Passing 200 feet AGL, flaps up in stages—ready to lower the nose if the engine quits—at 500 feet, power adjusted to climb and then boost pump off. I'll turn left now. I have terrain clearance and an airspeed margin. What a great day.

Chapter 5

Approach and Landing

Taildraggers teach threshold speed.

When landing a tail wheel airplane, a powered approach is the normal procedure because:
- you can positively control the rate of descent and flight path in varying winds;
- the engine is kept warm (ensuring power is available for a go-round) and clear of carburetor icing;
- there is more elevator power due to slipstream for the flare and so the airspeed can be lower; and
- the change of attitude in the flare is less than the flare for a glide approach.

The disadvantage is that you will not make it to the threshold if the engine fails. It is a balance between the risk of engine failure versus problems associated with a less controlled approach and landing. If your aircraft has an unreliable engine, the decision is clear. With a reliable engine, I would support the powered approach.

Airplane Control on Approach

Any approach begins with assessing the ground conditions, the approaches, the overshoot area, the surface wind and the wind gradient.

Remember the piloting formula?

$$Power\ (+\ configuration)\ +\ attitude = performance.$$

In practice, the pilot sets the power and configuration and uses attitude to control or vary the flight path and speed (performance is the combination of flight path and speed).

In the case of maneuvering relative to a feature on the ground, the formula becomes

$$power\ (+\ configuration)\ +\ attitude\ +\ wind\ velocity = ground\ path\ +\ ground\ speed$$

where *ground path* is the path relative to a point on the ground (the approach path angle and track).

This is an important factor to appreciate. It affects all low flying, and maneuvering relative to the ground, including takeoff and landing, and applies equally to small and large airplanes. For example, in low flying, we set power and attitude to produce a level flight path at a certain airspeed, but the direction and speed relative to the ground also depends very much on wind. Further, the *apparent* speed and path depends on movement relative to a point on the ground.

For a landing approach, we set power (and configuration) and attitude, and correct flight path and speed according to the performance relative to our aim point.

Power, configuration and attitude set on base determines the path through the air and the airspeed. Power must then be adjusted to compensate for wind. When power is adjusted, the attitude must also be changed and the aircraft trimmed. With experience (and a constant airspeed and configuration), the aim point on the runway can be placed at a certain spot on the windscreen and then tracked.

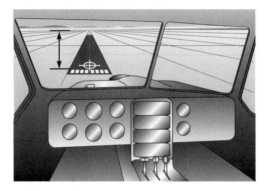

Figure 5-1. Runway aim point.

Why are we discussing the control in such detail? It is important to realize that the easy technique for the approach is to set the configuration and the power (with an allowance for the wind), set the attitude, and then fine-tune according to the relative movement of the aim point. We must start by knowing fairly accurately what power and attitude to set. This takes experience but, more importantly, good observation.

Decision to Land

There are many factors that should be considered in the pilot's decision-making process in deciding whether to go ahead with the landing at that field, at that time and on that particular runway, or to go around for another approach or on to another field. Factors that affect the landing performance of the airplane (the landing distance required) include:

- approach path;
- runway length;
- runway slope;
- runway surface;
- density altitude;
- wind velocity;
- wind gradient;
- turbulence;
- aircraft gross weight and CG position;

- aircraft configuration;
- aircraft age (engine and propeller);
- the pilot's familiarity with the field, the aircraft and the conditions; and, above all,
- whether there is a safe escape route for a go-around if the approach turns sour.

Approach Path

The landing performance of an aircraft depends on the final approach being at the correct speed and the correct angle. If there are obstacles, the approach path is steeper and the aim point has to be further into the field; thus, the landing distance would be increased. An attempt to duck under the approach path—to touchdown as early as possible—carries a risk of an airspeed increase and a higher rate of descent.

Runway Length

If necessary, consult the landing chart to confirm that the runway is adequate for the conditions and airplane weight. A touch-and-go landing requires additional length.

Runway Slope

Slope has significant effect—both for and against. Do not accept a downward-sloping runway unless there is a strong head wind. Watch out for high terrain in the overshoot climb area.

Runway Surface

Adverse factors for taxiing or takeoff may be in our favor for a landing. Long grass, wet grass, puddles and mud can help, provided they do not cause the wheels to skid or damage to the landing gear.

Density Altitude

High elevations and high temperatures decrease air density and increase the landing distance required (higher TAS and ground speed for the same threshold airspeed). They also reduce the power for a go-around and undermine climb performance, both rate and angle.

Wind Effects

Wind gradients and shear have been discussed in some detail (and in further detail below). As far as performance is concerned, the stronger the head wind on final approach, the better.

Aircraft Weight and CG Position

Increased weight means a higher approach speed (to maintain a safe margin above the increased stall speed). The energy that the brakes have to absorb in the landing roll is a function of weight and the square of the ground speed; therefore, weight has a compounding effect on landing distance required.

Rearward CG gives greatest control power. Forward CG makes the flare more difficult. Keep some power applied until after the start of the flare, then close the throttle.

Aircraft Configuration

Flaps provide:
- a lower stalling speed, thus permitting a lower approach speed while retaining a safe margin over the stall (usually $1.3V_S$);
- a steeper flight path at a given airspeed and power setting because of the increased drag;
- better flight path control and quicker response because of the balance between the higher drag and power;
- a lower nose attitude at a given airspeed, providing a better view of the approach and landing path; and
- a shorter float and a shorter landing run because of the increased drag and the lower airspeed.

The degree of flap will depend on the airplane and the wind conditions actually prevailing. In strong and gusty winds, it may be preferable to use less than full flap for better controllability and power response. Follow the advice in the pilot's operating handbook. Your flight instructor will show you the optimum technique for your airplane.

Aircraft Age and Condition

Aircraft condition is less critical for landing than for takeoff. However, the go-around is often a more critical maneuver than the takeoff. Make a value judgment that allows for some reduced performance for the go-around and allows a clear climb path. Tire and brake wear will obviously affect braking distance and steering. Deflated tires will slow you down more quickly, but will also cause directional problems.

Pilot Qualities and Familiarity

The pilot is the weakest link, but also the most crucial: the pilot determines the margin of control and therefore the margin of safety in the approach. The skill, anticipation, self-discipline, recent experience and professionalism of the pilot are the most important factors. Then comes experience and familiarity with the field, the airplane and the conditions. Ultimately, the pilot must decide the degree of risk to be taken but, for the sake of all on board, that risk should be minimized. This is within the pilot's power.

Escape Routes

Never commit to a landing unless you can safely go around from any point. Do not go beyond a nominated safe go-around point unless you are certain of a successful landing; once beyond this point, you are committed to land. When you establish this non-negotiable decision-point, it is go or no-go, no questions asked. Never defer this decision.

Atmospheric Effects

Wind Gradient

The wind usually increases in strength and changes direction as you move further away from the ground. Near the surface, the wind loses energy and slows down due to the friction with the ground and between the layers of air. This loss of energy causes the pressure gradient (high to low across the isobars, and vice versa) to be more pronounced and hence change the wind direction with changing altitude.

Any change in wind speed or direction with change in altitude is referred to as *wind shear*. We have differentiated between a gradual change as *wind gradient* and a sudden change as *wind shear*.

During an approach, small but virtually continuous changes of power and attitude will be required to maintain the desired flight path. Be ready to correct any tendency to go above or below the flight path (which leads to overshoot or undershoot). For example, consider an airplane approaching to land that descends from an overlying tail wind into calm conditions. The effect is similar to stepping from a moving train onto a stationary platform. Your body will want to maintain its original speed (speed of the train) due to its momentum, and your legs will have to move fast when they first touch the platform. No doubt, you will act quickly to adjust to the situation (maybe from a run to a walk).

In the same way, an airplane entering a new parcel of air will initially maintain its ground speed (due to its inertia). In our example, the new parcel of air is stationary, and the parcel exited was an overlying tail wind, thus the airspeed will show a sudden increase that the pilot will see on the airspeed indicator. (Ground speed is not displayed in light aircraft.)

With the sudden increase in airspeed, the nose of the airplane will tend to pitch up, and the temporarily improved performance will cause the airplane to move above the desired flight path. You would reduce power and adjust the pitch attitude to regain the desired airspeed (50 knots on the airspeed indicator) and flight path. Once back on speed and on slope, further adjustments of power and attitude will most likely be necessary: probably a small increase in power and a higher nose attitude to hold the airspeed and not go below slope.

Since the initial effect of the wind gradient, in this case, is to increase performance, this causes an overshoot in airspeed and/or flight path called the *overshoot effect*.

An *overshoot effect* will occur when an airplane flies into:
- a decreasing tail wind;
- an increasing head wind; or
- an updraft (e.g. a thermal).

An *undershoot effect* will occur when an airplane flies into:
- a decreasing head wind;
- an increasing tail wind (for instance, flying near the ground under a thundercloud); or
- in a downdraft (for instance, just under the base of a mature thunderstorm).

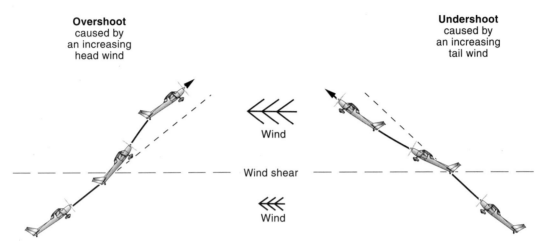

Figure 5-2. Climbing into an increasing wind.

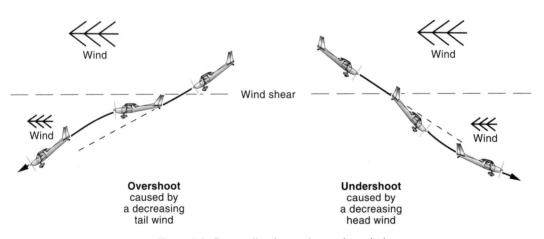

Figure 5-3. Descending into a decreasing wind.

For example, an airplane on approach to land with an airspeed of 70 knots descends from an overlying head wind into calm air. In this case, the airplane will lose 15 knots of airspeed as it passes through the wind gradient, its nose will tend to drop, and it will go below the desired flight path. Appropriate corrective action would be to add power and raise the nose to regain airspeed and the desired flight path, and then, when on speed and on slope, adjust the power and attitude as necessary.

Figure 5-4. Severe downdrafts beneath cumulonimbus (Cb) storm cloud.

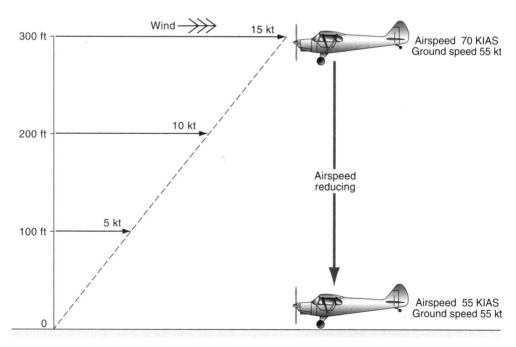

Figure 5-5. Descending into a decreasing wind.

Wind Shear

:ar has the greatest effect on an aircraft with a large momentum as they take a greater time to accelerate or decelerate. It is a less serious problem in light airplanes, although the turbulence and vertical gusts can effect control and performance more severely than a large aircraft.

Wind shear, the more sudden change of wind direction or speed at different levels, is reflected by a momentary airspeed change as the aircraft's momentum tries to maintain its previous ground speed until aerodynamic forces change the status quo; for example, the aircraft at an airspeed of 100 knots in a 30-knot head wind has a 70-knot ground speed (think of 30 knots of the airspeed being generated by the wind). As the aircraft climbs through the shear, it experiences a sudden wind change of 90°; the head wind becomes a crosswind. The momentum tries to hold the ground speed at 70 knots, but the 30-knot head wind comes off the bottom line—airspeed. It is now a balance between loss of lift and loss of drag. The aircraft will sink but, if it is light and if there is plenty of excess power, it will quickly accelerate to an airspeed of 100 knots. The effect is worst in aircraft with low drag change (a flat drag curve around the approach speed), little excess thrust and high momentum, hence the problem is worse for the large jets.

In light aircraft, the avoidance of known wind shear, and the automatic pilot reactions to changing speed by changing power as well as attitude, will maintain control.

Wind Gusts

A gusting wind has the same effect as shear. If the wind is changing from 20 to 40 knots, the gust factor is 20 knots (and the average is 30 knots plus or minus 10). If the pilot adds half of the gust factor, in this case 10 knots, to determine the fluctuation to a normal approach speed of, say, 60 knots and therefore flies the approach at 70 knots, then the airspeed fluctuation will be from 60 to 80 knots. If the 20 knots was added and the approach flown at 80 knots, the airspeed would fluctuate from 70 to 90 knots—all a little too fast. If no allowance was made, the airspeed would fluctuate from 50 to 70 knots—a little on the low side. Half the gust factor has proven to be a good compromise.

Turbulence

The best way to cope with turbulence is to set the power and fly attitude. The performance instruments (airspeed and rate of descent) will oscillate with the turbulence. Do not sweat over the numbers. Fly attitude and use the average reading of the instruments.

Air Density

The thickness of the air, on which we depend for lift and thrust, varies with pressure and temperature. The parameters are intimately interwoven. If we take a parcel of air and squash it, its pressure and temperature increase, as does its density; that is, the same amount of air is squeezed into a smaller space.

*More dense air gives more lift, more drag, greater stability
and greater control power. Less dense air gives less.*

The engine breathes air and so the pressure, temperature and density also affect its performance. Thrust reduces with reduced air density (the propeller has less mass to push), and the engine power output is reduced because there is less mass and less oxygen in each charge that is fired in the cylinders. In addition, high outside air temperatures (OAT) mean there is less temperature rise in combustion and so less power.

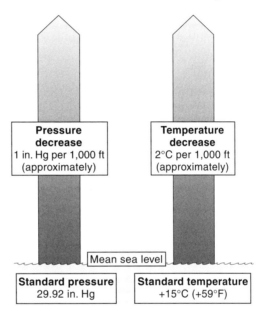

Figure 5-6. Standard atmospheric conditions.

Pressure decrease
1 in. Hg per 1,000 ft
(approximately)

Temperature decrease
2°C per 1,000 ft
(approximately)

Mean sea level

Standard pressure
29.92 in. Hg

Standard temperature
+15°C (+59°F)

To take these factors into account, we need a measure or scale. The performance charts for the aircraft use a parameter, which takes into account the effects of pressure, temperature and density. This is called *density altitude* (DA). It is the equivalent altitude in the standard atmosphere that has the same density of air that corresponds to these values at your elevation. Thus a density altitude of 4,000 feet means that the aircraft will behave as if it is actually at 4,000 feet in the standard atmosphere. For example, we could be taking off at an airfield that is 2,000 feet above sea level and the temperature may be 104°F (45°F or 25°C above the standard and therefore a much lower air density)—that is equivalent to being at about 5,000 feet altitude.

Aircraft performance is affected because we now have to travel at a higher TAS to achieve the same IAS and so the takeoff run, in particular, will be much longer. It is very useful to compare the performance of your aircraft in typical summer and winter conditions, and from airfields of various elevations. It is useful to know the ball-park figures.

Your charts may have a direct scale for density altitude or indirectly, for pressure altitude and temperature, which gives the same correction.

Flight Technique

Entry into the Pattern

Set power and attitude to achieve level flight as you join the pattern. Check the wind sock, listen and look for traffic and complete the prelanding checks. Now actually plan the downwind and base legs with an allowance for wind and wind gradient. Do not wait for the effect—anticipate.

Base Turn

The base turn position is the key reference point for commencing and judging the approach. It should be a consistent position relative to the aim point, for every approach, in any conditions, except abnormal operations (such as no flaps or no power). The base turn entry should be conducted in a set sequence of power, configuration, bank, attitude and trim. The aircraft is turned to a heading that allows for drift. Then the first assessment of the approach path is made and the power is adjusted—up or back.

Establishing the Approach Path

Eyeball the aim point early on the base leg and assess the view of the runway. Make an immediate power adjustment and/or lower more flap. Make corrections for drift also on the base leg so you are not blown away from the runway and forced to make a shallow approach. Assess any head or tail wind component and be prepared to turn earlier or later to intercept the runway centerline. In particular, avoid the situation where you turn late and find you are having to increase bank and pull the airplane around the turn. This can be a high-risk zone. If it feels uncomfortable, level the wings and go around.

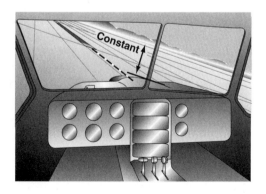

Figure 5-7. Turning final.

Establishing Centerline and Turning Onto Final Approach

Anticipate and allow for the effect of the wind in the final turn by commencing earlier or later and establishing a lesser or greater bank according to the crosswind effect.

Be wary of any tail wind component on the base leg as it will push you through the centerline and force you to tighten the final turn.

The aircraft is on the runway centerline when the centerline of the runway is perpendicular to the horizon. The aircraft does not necessarily point at the runway (because of wind) but it is positioned on the centerline.

Roll out on final with an allowance for crosswind. It is better to over-anticipate rather than wait to see the effect. Use the values in the following table as a guide and then fine-tune:

Approach Ground Speed (Knots)	Wind Correction Angle	
	10-Knot Crosswind	20-Knot Crosswind
60	10°	20°
90	7°	13°
120	5°	10°
150	3°	6°

Figure 5-8. Wind correction angle.

Note: If your approach ground speed is 90 knots and touchdown speed is 60 knots with a 20-knot crosswind, the wind correction angle in the flare increases from 13° to 20°. That is why the airplane starts to drift more just before touchdown. We will consider this more when we talk of crosswind landing techniques.

Final Approach

When straightened on the final approach carry out the final checks (I use *PUF*):
- *propeller*—full fine (carburetor heat cold, if appropriate);
- *undercarriage*—down, three greens; and
- *flaps*—full.

As the last stage of flap extends, adjust the attitude and power and retrim the airplane. Decide the type of landing you are going to do—three point or wheeler—as this determines your threshold speed. Now reduce to that speed and aim for a stabilized approach path, speed and attitude prior to the flare.

Having set the aircraft parameters, it is a matter of detecting movement of the aim point and making power, attitude and heading corrections to change the approach path and speed. *Aim point–attitude–airspeed* is a good work-cycle. At this low speed, it is important to make coordinated use of rudder with any aileron application (to overcome adverse aileron yaw).

We tend to think of a smooth pilot as a good pilot, and this is generally so; however, in some conditions, the pilot must be very active with the controls. Smoothness comes after achieving positive control (not instead of). Early, small and frequent corrections to attitude, heading and power produce a more stable flight path and speed. A gentler but slower response requires larger inputs and further corrections. It is better to overcorrect and allow too much rather than too little, too late.

Slipping

Let's be certain we are on the same wavelength with regard to our understanding of each of these flight maneuvers. Ultimately, the forward slip and sideslip produce the same result—high drag with crossed controls.

Forward Slip

A forward slip is a means of increasing drag and therefore steepening the approach path in any conditions. The aircraft is yawed away from runway heading and then banked toward the runway. The nose is lowered to maintain approach speed. The increased drag gives a steeper path and an increased rate of descent.

Sideslip

A sideslip is exactly the same as the so-called wing-down crosswind approach technique. When lined up on final approach, the into-wind wing is lowered and opposite rudder used to prevent yaw until the degree of bank counters the crosswind.

The end result is the same as the sideslip except the aircraft is pointing at the runway as distinct from tracking toward the runway. In nil wind, the airplane would deviate from the centerline.

Check if your airplane is approved for slips with the flaps extended: some are not and some have large airspeed indicator errors when slipping.

Slipping Turn

A slipping turn is a deliberately unbalanced turn again to increase drag and to lose altitude in the turn onto base leg or final approach. It consists of overbanking and using top rudder to prevent the nose dropping in to the turn. The drag is high due to the sideslip angle. Spitfire and Pitts pilots know the slipping turn well because it is also used to see ahead until the last minute on final approach.

Short Finals

A good landing follows a good approach, so aim to be stabilized, with the airplane accurately trimmed, before you reach short finals. Short finals for a GA airplane is the last 200 feet of height. Do not allow significant deviations in flight path, tracking or airspeed to develop. Small, quick, early corrections are the way to go. It is better to overcorrect initially and then smooth the responses rather than be chasing the right attitude, power and heading.

Carburetor heat will normally be returned to cold on short finals, in case maximum power is required for a go-around; however, if icing conditions exist, follow the guidance provided in your pilot's operating handbook.

Before landing, check the position of your feet and the brakes to avoid inadvertent braking on touchdown and to ensure both feet have the brakes available if needed.

Landing Technique

Pilot's Viewpoint

Judgment of the landing approach and flare is critically dependent on a consistent visual reference—both vertical and lateral.

Sitting Height

Your sitting height significantly affects your visual perception of the runway on landing. Always set the seat position and cushions to give the same view.

Side-By-Side Seating

If the pilot's eyes are not on the centerline of the aircraft, there will be a small error. It is not significant for most aircraft. The pilot's eyes are only 18 inches or so off-center and this amount cannot be discerned early in the approach. Pilots tend to overcorrect for offset seating and make matters worse. Place your eyes on the centerline until crossing the threshold. Then make a small correction, if you wish.

Landing Maneuver

Once the landing is assured (the momentum will carry the airplane to the threshold and the aircraft crosses the under-run), the aim point serves no further purpose. It is important now to look well ahead to judge the landing maneuver. The landing starts when the pilot's eyes are about 10–15 feet above the runway—for a light aircraft, that is. The height itself is reasonably tolerant as the pilot can adjust the rate of pitch in the flare to arrive at the hold-off height.

To commence the flare and to judge the rate of pitch to achieve an almost level path over the runway, the pilot uses cues, which include surface texture and detail (such as grass), the height of objects (trees or buildings), the width of the runway (very important but deceptive if you change from one runway to another of a different width) and the perceived height of the peripheral horizon (when the horizon feels right, especially the sides of your viewing area). It is very intuitive, being based on experience in a particular aircraft for a particular runway.

Leave the power set as you commence the flare, otherwise the loss of lift, reduced elevator power and the nose-down pitching moment all work against you.

Close the throttle once the flight path is near level and you can allow the aircraft to settle onto its main wheels and pinned for a wheeler, or be held off the ground until the aircraft is in the three-point attitude.

Taildragger in the Flare

Here there may be a significant difference between the taildragger and the tricycle. By its very nature a taildragger must have enough elevator power to hold the aircraft into the stall so that a three-point attitude can be achieved for touchdown. Your tricycle gear touring airplane may not be able to reach the stalling angle due to design-limited elevator travel. Many require considerable force to hold the aircraft off the ground in the flare; some cannot be held off when the throttle is closed. Because of the elevator power, there is a slight tendency to overcontrol in pitch when first landing a taildragger.

Types of Landing

With a tricycle gear, there is only one landing technique. For the taildragger, there are two major types and one variation:
- three-point;
- wheeler; and its variation,
- tail-down wheeler.

Three-Point Landing

The three-point landing is a minimum touchdown speed landing with the aircraft in the stall attitude so that all three wheels touch together. This is the normal landing for the taildragger as the aircraft is on the ground to stay (the wings are stalled and any gusts will not lift it back into the air). The landing roll is also the minimum.

Wheeler Landing

Occasionally, a landing is made at higher speed on the main wheels with the aircraft in a near-level attitude. The nose is lowered a little further on touchdown to reduce the angle of attack to prevent any bounce. The wheeler landing offers more control because of the higher speed airflow over the control surfaces. This is valuable in gusty crosswind conditions. The view ahead is also better and, in some aircraft, the tail can be kept up until late in the landing roll. However, be careful with the reduced propeller clearance.

The disadvantages of the wheeler are the higher speed (longer landing roll) and the vulnerability of the aircraft as the tail settles. The rudder loses effect before the tail wheel touches down. The usual wheeler is a controlled touchdown with the aircraft still flying above the stall and the aircraft in a near-level attitude. Thus the angle of attack has to be reduced on touchdown by raising the tail or at least preventing it from dropping. The threshold speed is typically 10 knots above the threshold speed for a three-point landing.

Tail-Down Wheeler

Some aircraft, especially larger aircraft such as the DC-3, respond better to a controlled touchdown with a little more speed and control response than that offered by the fully stalled, three-point landing. However, the level wheeler might not appropriate because of the longer landing roll and the more difficult transition to the tail-down attitude.

The compromise is the tail-down wheeler. This compromise landing has a slightly higher speed than the three-point landing and the aircraft is allowed to touch down before the three-point attitude. The attitude is checked forward and held. The tail drops shortly after as the throttles are closed and the propwash decays. The control is then held back to improve steering.

Technique

A normal landing (three-point) is similar to the approach to the stall in level flight, with attitude being increased to keep the aircraft flying as the airspeed decays. Touchdown will occur just prior to the moment of stall. Do not rush and try not to be tense. The aircraft will land when it is ready.

The landing consists of four phases:
1. flare (or round-out);
2. hold-off;
3. touchdown; and
4. ground roll.

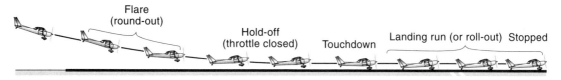

Figure 5-9. The landing.

1. Flare

During the flare (round-out) the nose is gradually raised to reduce the rate of descent. The descent rate is checked by a slight attitude change (only 3°) with the pitch rate adjusted to suit: a high rate of sink requiring a greater and quicker backward movement. A high sink rate may require the pilot to add power momentarily to arrest the descent.

To assist in judging the height of the wheels above the ground and the rate at which the airplane is sinking, your eyes should be looking well ahead from shortly before commencing the flare (when airspeed is no longer important) until the end of the landing run.

To achieve the best depth perception and develop a feel for just where the main wheels are in relation to the ground, it is best to look to the far end of the runway. You use peripheral vision to assist height and path judgment, but the center of attention is the far end of the runway. Even when it disappears behind the engine cowl, the runway sides indicate the point of convergence.

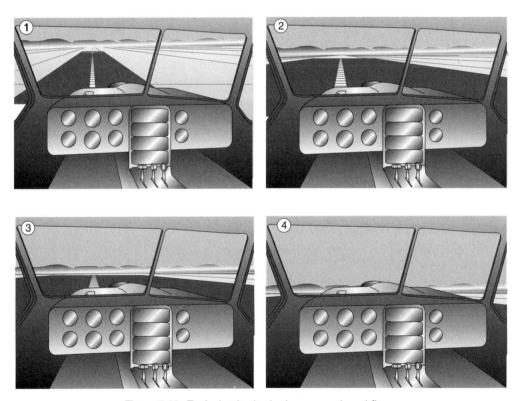

Figure 5-10. Typical attitudes in the approach and flare.

2. Hold-Off

The hold-off should occur with the airplane close to the ground (the wheels within a foot or so). The throttle is slowly closed (unless the field length is critical) and the control column is progressively brought back to keep the airplane flying a level path with the wheels just off the ground. If sinking, apply more back pressure; if moving away from the ground, relax the back pressure. Look well ahead of the nose.

You should be looking well ahead from the beginning of round-out until touchdown. Any sideways drift is counteracted by lowering the into-wind wing a few degrees and keeping the aircraft pointing straight with rudder.

3. Touchdown

For a wheeler, allow the wheels to touch as soon as the flight path is level by making no further movement of the stick. As soon as the wheels touch, check the control forward to stick the wheels on and to prevent the tail dropping (which would increase the angle of attack of the wing and the aircraft would bounce back into the air).

For a three-point landing, hold the aircraft in the air until it cannot be held-off any longer.

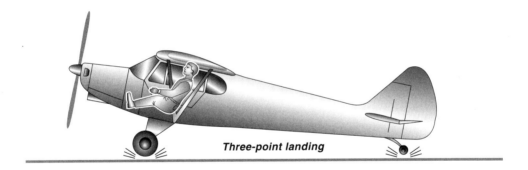

Three-point landing

Landing bottom (butt) first or
keeping your feet off the ground

Figure 5-11. Holding off—ideal.

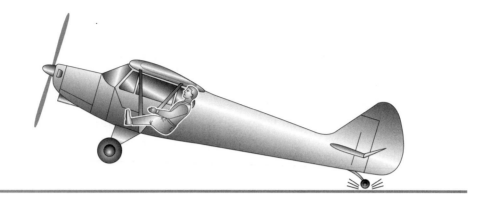

Figure 5-12. Holding off—too slow (some aircraft are possible to land tail wheel first, especially if the pilot flies from the rear seat and flapless).

4. Ground Roll

During the ground roll, the airplane is kept running straight down the centerline using rudder and the wings are kept level (prevented from lifting) with aileron. Hold the stick back firmly to keep the tail wheel on the ground and to improve directional control. Brakes may be used once the tail wheel is on the ground, or even before if you are careful.

Remember that the landing is not complete until the end of the landing run when the airplane is stationary or has exited the runway at taxiing speed.

Common Faults in the Landing

Every pilot learns how to land by experience—it comes with practice and repetition. It is inevitable that many landings will be less than perfect, but they can be consistently safe and controlled.

Common faults are:
- the *balloon* (when the airplane moves away from the ground due to over-rotation before touchdown);
- the *bounce* (when it moves away from the ground after touchdown, perhaps after several touchdowns, due to overcontrol after touchdown); and
- the *hang-up* (hung-up with reducing airspeed).

Balloon

A balloon can be caused by either:
- too much or too sudden back pressure on the control column; and/or
- too much power left on; and/or
- too high an airspeed; and/or
- a gust of wind.

To correct for a small balloon:
- relax some of the back pressure on the control column;
- allow the airplane to commence settling (sinking) again;
- when approaching the hold-off height, resume the backward movement of the control column (if a rate of sink has developed add power also); and
- complete the touchdown normally.

Some runway will have been consumed in the process so keep an eye on the runway distance remaining.

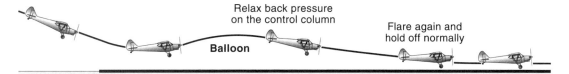

Figure 5-13. Correcting for a small balloon.

A large balloon may call for a go-around, certainly for an inexperienced pilot. As experience is gained, it may be possible to reposition the airplane (possibly using power) for the flare and landing, but this uses up lots of runway. The decision to attempt a recovery from a large flare will therefore depend on the extent of your experience and on the runway length remaining.

Bounced Landing

A bounce can be caused by:
- failing to flare sufficiently (touching down with vertical speed); and/or
- touching down too fast; and/or
- touching down on the main wheels but not stopping the tail from settling; and/or
- backward movement of the control column on touchdown; and/or
- flaring too high and then sinking rapidly.

An inexperienced pilot should consider an immediate go-around following a bounce. With experience, however, a successful recovery from a bounce can be made (provided that the runway length is adequate) by relaxing the back pressure and adding power if necessary to reposition the airplane suitably to recommence the landing. Avoid pushing the nose down as a second bounced touchdown may result.

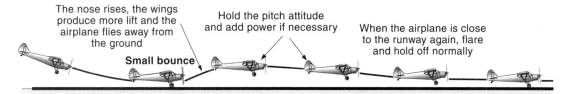

Figure 5-14. Recovery from a bounced landing.

Prior to touchdown, make sure that the airplane is in the correct nose-high attitude (even if it is the second touchdown).

Hang-Up

A hang-up results from over-rotating in the flare (ballooning), and allowing the aircraft to climb with reducing airspeed. This may occur when not responding quickly to a bounce, or from simply flaring and holding off too high.

Flaring and Holding Off Too High

The hold-off is best completed with the main wheel tires within a foot or less of the ground. Any more than this and the result will be either a heavier-than-usual landing, or a prolonged hold-off that leads to a stall with subsequent, severe drop to the ground.

Before impact, if you recognize that you are too high, hold the attitude and add power; this will break the descent rate somewhat and allow a less heavy touchdown. Immediately as the wheels touch the ground, close the throttle, otherwise the airplane may not decelerate.

Holding off too high usually results from either:
- not looking far enough ahead, with the result that estimation of the flight path is poor; or
- a second attempt to land following a balloon or bounce.

If control ever becomes marginal, apply full power and go around.

Full Stop, Stop-and-Go or Touch-and-Go?

A normal landing brings the aircraft to a full stop. For training purposes, to save time and money, some variations are used. These are the stop-and-go and the touch-and-go. The stop-and-go consists of a landing to a full stop on the runway followed by an immediate takeoff using the remaining length of the runway. It can only be done on runways of adequate length for both the landing and the takeoff. Moreover, the runway is occupied for a prolonged period and other traffic may be affected.

The touch-and-go is a continuous maneuver where, after the touchdown, the power is increased before the airplane stops and the aircraft enters a continuous takeoff. In some aircraft, it is necessary to retrim and to retract flaps during this maneuver. Again, it can only be done safely on runways with enough length for the landing, the change of configuration and trim, the introduction of power and the subsequent takeoff. The workload during a touch-and-go is higher than a normal landing.

For a taildragger the transition from landing and decelerating to immediately accelerating and taking-off again is a demanding exercise, and so to be approached with caution. I prefer not to use the practice for training inexperienced pilots.

Chapter 6

Advanced Takeoffs and Landings

There are several factors that may make the takeoff and landing more demanding than usual. The wind is not always gentle, nor always straight down the runway. Not all strips and fields are perfect in terms of length, width, definition, surface, slope, direction, approaches and over-runs. We have called these operations *advanced*.

Crosswind

Not all airfields have a runway that faces into the wind on a given day. Some are so constrained by terrain that they are built out of alignment with the prevailing wind. Every airplane type (even a Boeing 747) has a maximum demonstrated crosswind component specified by the manufacturer or operator. If the actual crosswind exceeds the limit for your airplane, or your own personal limit (in that airplane, on that day, under those weather conditions, at that weight and at that airfield), then use a different runway or divert to another airfield.

Crosswind Component

The crosswind component on a runway can be estimated from the wind strength and the angle that the wind direction makes with the runway.

As a guide:
- a wind 30° off the runway has a crosswind component of ½ the wind speed;
- a wind 45° off the runway has a crosswind component of approximately 70% the wind speed;
- a wind 60° off the runway has a crosswind component of approximately 85% the wind speed.

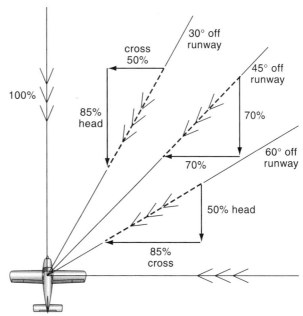

Figure 6-1. Estimating crosswind component.

73

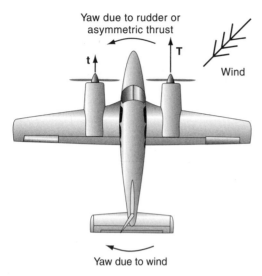

Yaw due to rudder or asymmetric thrust

Wind

Yaw due to wind

Figure 6-2. Asymmetric thrust may be used to assist rudder power.

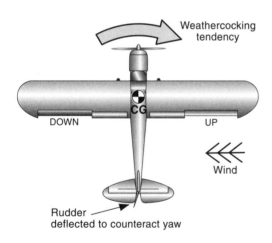

Weathercocking tendency

DOWN   UP

Wind

Rudder deflected to counteract yaw

Wind

Aileron to keep the wings level

Figure 6-3. Keep straight with rudder; level wings with ailerons.

Crosswind Flight Technique

Crosswind Takeoff

Weathercocking and Wing Lifting

In a crosswind, the airplane will tend to weathercock into the wind because of the large keel surfaces behind the main wheels. Furthermore, the upwind wing will want to lift. Provided that the crosswind limit for your airplane is not exceeded, it will be possible to maintain control. The crosswind restriction may be due to a limit in directional control (rudder power) or lateral control (aileron power). All airplanes eventually reach a limit of aileron power, and may reach a point where the pilot cannot hold a wing down, possibly before reaching the directional control limit.

Whether the airplane reaches its rudder or aileron limit first depends on the landing gear track, whether the aircraft has a high or low wing, wing loading, aspect ratio, the size and maximum deflection of the rudder and ailerons, flap position, and CG position. This determines the symptoms and control inputs required for that particular airplane. It is a matter of knowing your airplane at its crosswind limit. In an multi-engine airplane, asymmetric thrust may be used to assist rudder power, but again this is a matter of knowing the airplane.

Lifting of the Upwind Wing

A crosswind will try to lift the upwind wing. While full aileron deflection should be applied early in the takeoff run, this can be reduced as the faster airflow increases control power. You do not have to consciously think of aileron movement; just apply more, rather than less, until it has effect, then concentrate on stopping the wing-lifting tendency.

Diagonal Takeoff Run

It is customary and standard practice to line up on the center of the runway and to track as best you can along the runway centerline. In a light airplane with very low crosswind limits and low takeoff speeds, or on marginal runways (length or width), it is worth considering a modified takeoff path that makes use of the increased diagonal length of the runway and the effective widening of the runway that this offers. This provides extra room to allow for the wind curving the aircraft's takeoff path.

Drift After Liftoff

As the airplane enters the air mass on liftoff, it will tend to move sideways with it, and to weathercock into the direction of the wind. Allow it to do so. But keep the wings level as it yaws. Do not allow the airplane to sink back onto the ground with drift. Avoid the massive sideloads that can damage the landing gear. For this reason, hold the airplane firmly on the ground during the ground

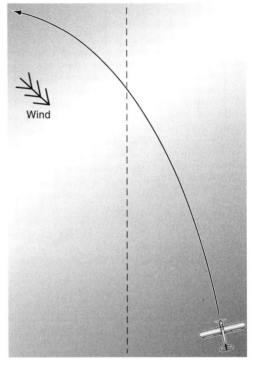

Figure 6-4. Lining up off center.

run (with slight forward pressure on the control column to hold a slightly negative angle of attack) and then lift off cleanly and positively. It may be advisable to delay liftoff until 5 knots or so past the normal rotation speed to achieve a clean liftoff.

1. Hold the airplane firmly on the runway (slight forward pressure); apply aileron into the wind to keep the wings level, and rudder to stay on the centerline.

2. Lift off cleanly and establish the climb attitude.

3. Remove 'crossed controls' as you yaw into wind to allow for drift.

4. Normal climb-out, maintaining the extended runway centerline by allowing for drift

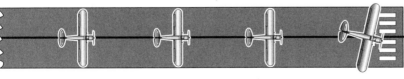

Figure 6-5. Crosswind takeoff.

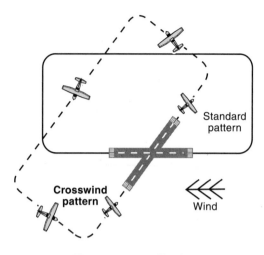

Figure 6-6. Lay off drift to maintain a rectangular pattern.

Crosswind Pattern

When flying a crosswind pattern, adjustments should be made to allow for the wind effect in the pattern, by allowing for drift and by modifying bank in the turns. Since the wind at pattern altitude may differ from ground level, use ground features to assist in tracking around the pattern.

In the pattern, a tail wind on the crosswind leg will tend to carry you wide on downwind. A head wind will keep you too close in. Adjust each leg of the pattern to compensate for drift and to give yourself room to maneuver. Try to follow the same path over the ground as you would on a calm day. It is better to slightly over-compensate for wind than under-compensate.

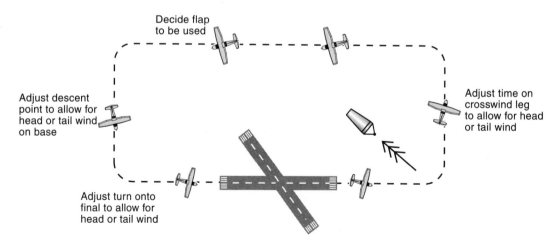

Figure 6-7. Flying the crosswind pattern.

Base Leg

Planning for the crosswind approach and landing starts with a real assessment of the wind on the surface and at pattern altitude and the effects associated with the wind such as potential turbulence and downdrafts. It also entails planning the approach and anticipating the effect of wind on the base leg and final approach, and during the landing flare and touchdown.

A tail wind on the base leg will increase your ground speed and tend to carry you through the runway centerline. Anticipate this by:

- setting power less than normal (about 100 RPM or 1 in. Hg MP less per 10 knots of wind), but be ready to adjust for the final approach;
- begin the turn onto the final approach early;
- establish the full amount of bank early (30 degrees); and
- continue the turn through the centerline to allow for drift on the final approach.

If you fly through centerline, avoid any tendency to overbank. (A bank angle of 30° is a reasonable maximum.) Simply continue the turn and join the final approach from the other side.

A head wind on the base leg will decrease your ground speed, so:

- carry a little more power;
- delay the turn onto the final approach and establish less bank; and
- roll out before runway heading to allow for drift.

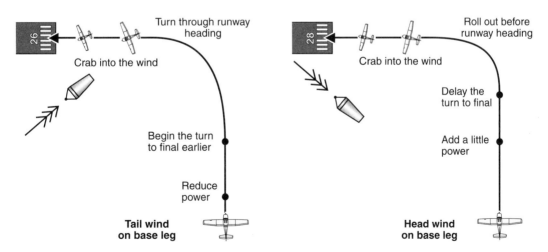

Figure 6-8. Allow for wind effect when turning onto final approach.

Final Approach

Centerline

Because of the wind correction angle needed to maintain the centerline, the runway will appear to one side of the nose, but the runway will still appear symmetrical. On final approach for a crosswind landing, you should have a view directly down the runway centerline. If the airplane drifts downwind, then make a very definite turn into the wind and regain final without delay. (Do not just aim the nose of the airplane at the runway.) Keep the airplane in balance.

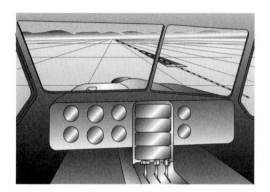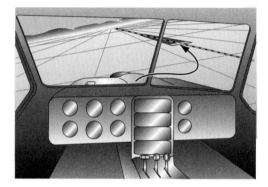

Figure 6-9. Correct any lateral displacement early on final approach.

Wind strength often decreases near the ground, so continual adjustments to heading will have to be made to maintain your track down the final approach. This is especially the case in strong and gusty conditions.

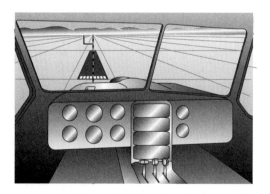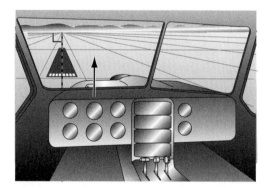

Figure 6-10. An into-wind approach and a crosswind approach, both on centerline.

Once tracking is under control, achieving a stabilized descent path and a controlled landing becomes a simpler task. It is particularly true in a crosswind that a good landing results from a stabilized approach.

General Considerations

Strong crosswinds are often accompanied by gusts and turbulence, and consideration should be given to using partial or zero flap and a slightly higher approach speed than normal to give better controllability.

The flare in a crosswind landing is normal, but the hold-off should not be prolonged (otherwise drift will develop). The airplane should be placed on the ground, wheels aligned with the runway, while the flight controls are effective and with the airplane tracking along the runway centerline. For this reason, many pilots prefer a wheeler landing in crosswind conditions.

Once on the ground, directional control is more easily achieved if the tail wheel is lowered onto the ground and the control column held back. You must maintain firm control throughout the whole maneuver until the airplane is stopped or exited the runway.

Hold the wing down with progressive into-wind aileron as the airspeed decreases (the crosswind will tend to lift the into-wind wing). Full into-wind control displacement may be required by the end of the landing run.

Landing Techniques

A touchdown with drift could cause structural damage or even tip the airplane over. The objectives in a crosswind landing are to:
- align the axis of the airplane (i.e. the main wheels) with the runway prior to touch-down;
- avoid any drift across the runway before the wheels touch down (that is, touch down on or close to the runway centerline before sideways motion develops); and
- prevent the upwind wing from lifting, or the tail yawing, as the aircraft slows.

This requires the coordinated use of all the primary controls (ailerons, rudder, elevator and power) and sometimes very active pilot inputs.

There are three accepted crosswind landing techniques:
- the crab method;
- the wing-down method; and
- the combination method, being a combination of a crabbed approach with a transition to a wing-down touchdown (incorporating the best features of each of the above).

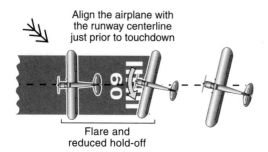

Align the airplane with
the runway centerline
just prior to touchdown

Flare and
reduced hold-off

Figure 6-11. In crab method, align
the airplane just prior to touchdown.

Crab Method

In the crab method, drift should be laid off all the way down the final approach and through the flare. This will keep the airplane tracking down the centerline, but the wheels will not be aligned with the landing direction.

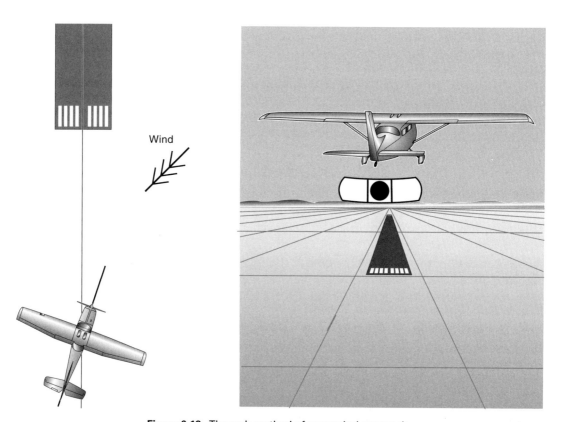

Wind

Figure 6-12. The crab method of crosswind approach.

Just prior to touchdown, yaw the airplane straight. Simultaneously apply opposite aileron to prevent the wing lifting. Then, before any sideways motion can develop, lower the into-wind wing until the wheel touches (this effectively becomes the combination method). Keep the aileron applied and even increase the amount as the aircraft slows. Note that the wind correction angle increases with reducing ground speed.

Approach ground speed (knots)	Wind correction angle	
	10-knot crosswind	20-knot crosswind
60	10°	20°
90	7°	13°
120	5°	10°
150	3°	6°

Figure 6-13. Increasing wind correction angle.

Wing-Down Method

The wing-down method is a slipping approach. It is sometimes recommended for high-wing aircraft that are susceptible to the into-wind wing being lifted or for aircraft where the rudder power is limited. Check your aircraft's flight manual. Some pilots prefer it.

Note the aircraft is slipping and so is not balanced. (Some passengers feel uncomfortable while slipping.) Moreover, the tilted wing (reduced vertical lift vector) means a steeper path and higher rate of descent. The flare needs to be initiated a little earlier for this reason.

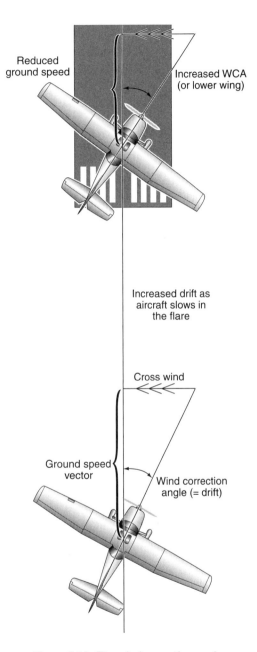

Figure 6-14. The wind correction angle increases with reducing ground speed.

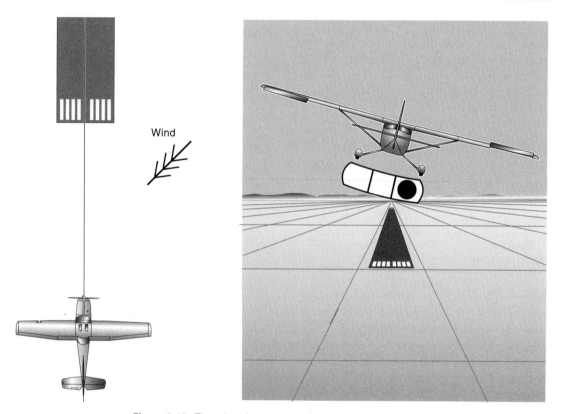

Wind

Figure 6-15. The wing-down crosswind approach technique.

To initiate a forward slip:
• lower the into-wind wing; and
• apply opposite rudder to stop the airplane turning and to keep its longitudinal axis aligned with the runway centerline.

The airplane is out of balance and so the skid ball will not be centered. The stronger the crosswind, the more wing-down and the more opposite rudder required.

Drift Control. If the airplane starts to drift downwind of the centerline, you have applied insufficient bank, so:
• lower the wing further; and
• keep straight with additional rudder.

If the airplane starts to slip upwind of the centerline, you have applied too much bank, so:
• reduce the bank; and
• keep straight with reduced rudder.

In gusty conditions especially, you will be continually varying the degree of wing–down and opposite rudder to remain aligned with the runway centerline. During this whole process adjust the pitch attitude to maintain airspeed. In some airplanes, the airspeed indicator misreads when slipping. Some aircraft are not approved for slips with the flaps extended. Check your airplane handbook.

Touchdown. The bank and opposite rudder is maintained through the flare and perhaps until touchdown on one wheel. The bank does need to be increased slightly as the airplane slows. When the upwind main wheel touches, there may be a tendency for the airplane to yaw into the wind, but the airplane can easily be kept straight with rudder. Keep the aileron applied. Less judgment and timing is required in the actual touchdown using the wing-down method, since the airplane is aligned with the centerline throughout the flare. There is no crab angle to remove and no sideways drift.

Figure 6-16. View from the cockpit in a left crosswind.

Combination Method

A distinct disadvantage of the wing-down technique being used all the way down the final approach is that the controls are crossed and the airplane is out of balance (that is, the ball is not centered). It is both inefficient and uncomfortable, as well as the rate of descent being higher. It is more difficult to judge the aircraft's attitude and aim point in a slipping approach. Larger aircraft, with swept wings, expose themselves to a risk of scraping the engine pods on landing. Light airplanes with high aspect ratio wings and narrow landing gear risk contacting the wing tip.

A more comfortable approach can be flown by crabbing until the flare. During the flare, the aircraft is straightened with rudder and the upwind wing is lowered simultaneously to prevent drift. This is the combination method.

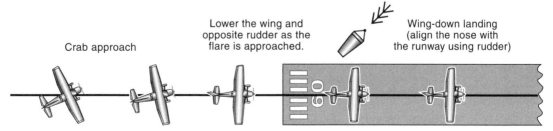

Crab approach
Lower the wing and opposite rudder as the flare is approached.
Wing-down landing (align the nose with the runway using rudder)

Figure 6-17. The combination (recommended) method of crosswind landing.

If The Wing Lifts In The Flare

You may find that some airplanes are easy to land in a crosswind until they are on the ground and then you realize you have not enough aileron power to stop the upwind wing lifting. If this happens you have two choices to regain control:

- apply power and accelerate to flying speed (go around); or
- in some cases allow the airplane to yaw into the wind and even help it around (obviously you need a wide runway or field to allow for this maneuver).

For this reason, if the conditions are marginal, it is worth considering a touchdown on the downwind edge of the strip to allow room for this.

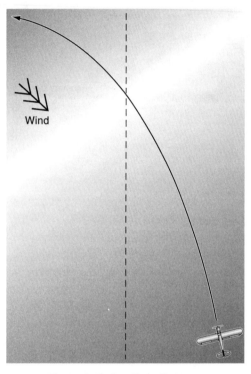

Wind

Figure 6-18. Landing off center.

Diagonal Landing

An aircraft with a very restricted crosswind limit, limited control power or on a short but wide runway can offset the limitation by making use of the diagonal length. This maximizes the landing distance that can be utilized. A normal approach is made parallel to the runway centerline but aligned to the downwind edge/side of the strip. This then allows for the aircraft to be turned partly into the wind after touchdown and then provides the maximum length of run available.

Short-Field Operations

A short field is one at which the runway length available and/or the obstacle-clearance gradients are only just sufficient to satisfy takeoff and landing requirements.

Performance Charts (P-charts)

The takeoff and landing performance charts for your airplane should be consulted to ensure that the runway length or obstacle clearance is adequate for the planned operations under the existing conditions. Allow also for downdrafts on the lee side of terrain. An inspection on foot of the proposed takeoff and landing surface and the surrounding area may be necessary.

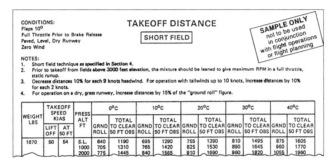

Figure 6-19. Consult the performance charts.

Eyeballing the Slope

Some agricultural pilots have a technique for judging the slope. Pick an object or a mark on the ground that is level with your eyes—your visual horizon if the ground was level. Then pace it out. If you are six feet tall and then you pace the distance to a point that is level with your eyes, and it is 60 paces away, the slope is 6 in 60, which is 6°—way too much for takeoff. Having measured the slope, it can be used as a reference to judge the climb gradient required. During the inspection remember that the takeoff is not complete until all obstacles are cleared in the climb-out, so not only the takeoff surface but also the surrounding area, needs to be considered.

Short-Field Takeoff

There are two major considerations for the short-field takeoff:
- minimizing the ground roll; and
- maximizing the initial climb angle.

To achieve the shortest ground run and steepest climb:
- take off into the wind or, if the surface wind is calm, into the wind gradient;
- use the optimum flap setting (as recommended by the manufacturer);

- ensure that the takeoff run is started as close to the end of the strip as possible (use the diagonal length if appropriate);
- apply power with brakes applied, holding the control column back to avoid damage to the propeller, releasing the brakes as full power is reached (although, if loose stones could damage the propeller, a rolling start is preferred);
- raise the tail to the level attitude as soon as the aircraft is moving forward;
- avoid braking to keep straight;
- lift off at the minimum recommended flying speed;
- select the nose attitude for the best angle-of-climb speed (fly V_X); and
- at a safe height, accelerate to normal climb speed and then retract the flaps.

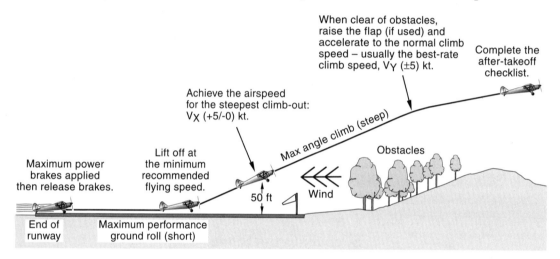

Figure 6-20. The short-field takeoff.

Short-Field Landing

The short-field landing is a landing with minimum ground run and, perhaps, maximum approach path angle if there are obstacles in the undershoot area. It is used when the strip:
- is of marginal length;
- has a surface or obstructions that restrict the usable length; or
- the undershoot requires a steep approach.

Approach and land as close as possible directly into the wind for a steeper approach path, lowest ground speed and shortest ground run. Full flap is preferred if wind conditions are suitable (no significant gusts). This allows the minimum approach speed, best forward view and maximum drag, and therefore less float prior to touchdown and most deceleration.

Position the airplane for a normal approach with an aim point as close to the threshold as practicable—even short of the threshold for critical fields, but watch for fences in the undershoot area. Fly as slow an approach speed as is safe (perhaps $1\cdot15V_S$ instead of $1\cdot3V_S$).

Check your pilot's operating handbook and plan a three-point landing. Set the attitude to achieve the desired airspeed and adjust the power to achieve the aim point. You are on the back side of the power curve (the back side of the drag curve) so active adjustments to power and attitude will be required to maintain the approach path and airspeed.

Obstacles in the approach path may require that an aim point further into the short field be chosen. Having cleared the obstacles, do not lower the nose dramatically or reduce power suddenly, otherwise a high sink rate and a heavy touchdown may result. Play it carefully. Intercept the normal path before crossing the threshold.

STEEP APPROACH PATH

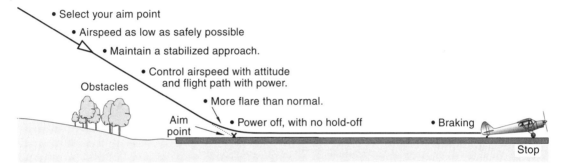

- Select your aim point
  - Airspeed as low as safely possible
    - Maintain a stabilized approach.
      - Control airspeed with attitude and flight path with power.

Obstacles

- More flare than normal.

Aim point
- Power off, with no hold-off
- Braking

Stop

Figure 6-21. Clear all obstacles in the approach path.

Aim to cross the airfield boundary at the selected speed and at the minimum safe height with power on. Close the throttle and reduce the rate of descent but do not flare fully. Do not prolong the hold-off. Allow the plane to touchdown; brake as required holding the stick back firmly. Since the nose will be higher due to the lower speed and higher power, a lesser attitude change will be required for the flare. Touchdown will follow immediately once the throttle is closed.

The airplane will touch down without float as soon as the throttle is closed. Do not hold it off the ground. This is a three-point, near-stalled landing. With the tail down, apply full back stick and firm braking. Be ready to yaw severely to avoid obstacles.

If a high sink rate develops add power to prevent a heavy landing. Power may be required all the way to the ground. If so, close the throttle as soon as the wheels touch.

Soft-Field Operations

A soft field is an area that has a surface such as sand or snow, a wet grassy surface, standing pools of water, or a rough, loose, stone or gravel surface. A soft field may be quite long with no obstacle-clearance problems in the climb-out or approach path. It may also be short, which means the short-field considerations and obstacle clearance may be important.

Soft surfaces create extra friction and stress on the wheels and therefore degrade the acceleration in the takeoff run. The wheels may have a dangerous tendency to dig in but, with full power, the elevators are powerful.

Soft-Field Takeoff

The main concern in a soft-field takeoff is to transfer the weight from the wheels to the wings as soon as possible, minimizing ground pressure and reducing the friction on the wheels. Consequently, optimum flap and maximum power should be used. The tail wheel should be raised as soon as possible and, as speed increases, back pressure is applied to lift the weight off the main wheels by degree. There will be some drag due to the deflected elevators, but this should be less than the friction on the wheels.

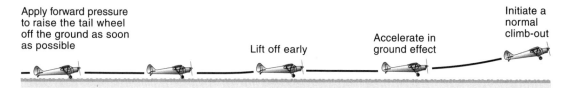

Figure 6-22. The soft-field takeoff.

Lift the airplane off the ground as soon as possible (minimum flying speed) and accelerate to climb speed in ground effect. Do not climb more than about 10 feet above the ground until a safe flying speed is attained.

Soft-Field Landing

Since the tendency on a soft field is for the main wheels to dig in, the aim should be to:
• land as slowly as possible (three-point landing); and
• hold the stick back during the landing roll.

Use full flap and fly a short-field (minimum speed) approach.

Unless you know the field, it is better to avoid landing on a soft surface. Consider also that you may not be able to takeoff again until it dries out. If the tires grab and the tail comes up, consider yawing the aircraft for a deliberate ground loop.

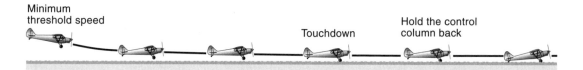

Figure 6-23. Soft-field landing.

Chapter 7

Low Flying

Why Fly at a Low Level?

Low level is generally considered to be below 500 feet above ground level (AGL). However, in practice the considerations should apply whenever we descend below 1,500 feet AGL, especially during takeoff and landing when we are most vulnerable.

At times, we may be maneuvering at low level to avoid a low ceiling or rain showers, or to inspect a landing area or perhaps power lines or pipelines. Other planes are used at low level for fire spotting and surveillance.

Ground-Referenced Flight

When flying low, we are flying with reference to ground features whereas normal flight uses ground features only for navigation (other than the visual horizon of course). In normal flight, the pilot uses the flight instruments to interpret flight path and speed. When flying low, the pilot has to spend most of the time looking out, and what the pilot sees can be deceptive. The pilot's eyes will see the ground going by. This relative motion may delude the pilot into reading the cues as airspeed and flight path, which they are not. This awareness is important as the cues affect the pilot's judgment. The eyes perceive the result of both flight path and wind; that is, they see ground speed and drift. The pilot must make a conscious effort to maintain airspeed and attitude as primary flight references, and use ground features for positioning rather than flying.

Speed

Airspeed is what the wing needs. However, the pilot's eyes perceive rate of progress over the ground—ground speed. The pilot can be tricked into thinking the airspeed is high when flying downwind and therefore unwisely reduce power. Many have crashed as a result.

Apparent Drift

As the airplane turns over the ground across the wind, the pilot perceives the track over the ground as an apparent sideways motion, perceived as slipping into or skidding out of the turn radius. There is a temptation to change the angle of bank and apply back pressure to correct this false slip/skid.

Pilots have stalled the airplane trying to prevent outward skid by pulling the airplane into a tighter turn. Allow room for the downwind drift before entering the turn so you do not have to pull it around, especially at low airspeed.

Inertia and Momentum

Momentum is the tendency of a moving object to continue at a constant speed in a straight line. The magnitude of an object's momentum is a function of the speed and direction relative to the earth not to the air; that is, it is ground speed and track made good that determine momentum.

Inertia is the reluctance of a stationary object to be moved or to have its direction changed. It also happens with respect to rotary motion; that is, a body resists change to its state of rest or steady rotary motion. This is called its *moment of inertia*.

This is expressed in Newton's second law of motion: a body continues in its state of rest or uniform motion in a straight line unless acted upon by an external force. The tendency or the power of the tendency to continue in a straight line at a particular speed is a function of its mass (m) and its speed (V).

Mathematically:

$$momentum = mV$$

Because the aircraft moves through the air, and that air may be moving, the aircraft's momentum is a function of heading, airspeed and wind velocity, i.e. ground speed and track.

A turn at constant airspeed will result in a changing momentum as the aircraft changes from upwind to downwind. Conversely, since the tendency to maintain speed and direction is a function of ground speed, the aircraft's airspeed will momentarily change as it adjusts to a new steady-state condition.

Let's say the aircraft is tracking directly downwind about to turn crosswind. The airspeed is 100 knots and the wind speed is 30 knots, so the airplane has a ground speed of 130 knots. As it turns, the ground speed will tend to stay at 130 knots but, as the relative wind direction changes, the airspeed will tend to increase. However, the drag will also rise and, with constant thrust, will stop any airspeed change unless the aircraft has great mass. Where the momentum is higher, the airspeed adjustment will take longer. This is why larger aircraft suffer more from the effects of wind shear.

If, instead, the aircraft was heading into the same wind, with an airspeed of 100 knots, the ground speed would be 70 knots. As the aircraft turns crosswind, the airspeed will tend to reduce. The drag will reduce and the aircraft will tend to accelerate to maintain the aerodynamic status quo; that is, the airspeed will increase. However, if the aircraft is heavy and if it is on the back end of the drag curve, it will not be able to compensate for the airspeed decay without additional thrust.

Acceleration (speed change) is the result of the applied force (thrust) and the mass of the aircraft ($F = ma$). Thus the heavier the aircraft, the greater the thrust change required to accelerate. The consequences for a big aircraft can be very serious with both airspeed loss and an increasing rate of descent.

A similar situation arises when the aircraft climbs or descends through a wind gradient (where the wind velocity changes with changing altitude). See figures 7-1 and 7-2.

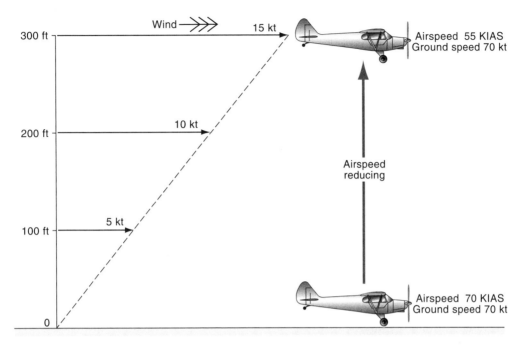

Figure 7-1. Effect of wind gradient when climbing downwind.

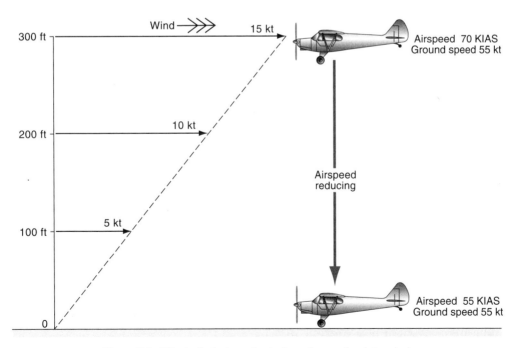

Figure 7-2. Effect of wind gradient when descending into wind.

Momentum and the Wing

The wing allows us to fly. It generates lift as a result of airspeed and angle of attack. If we take away the airspeed, the lift disappears. Lift is proportional to the square of the airspeed. If airspeed is halved, the lift is reduced to one-quarter of its previous value.

If momentum suddenly reduces the airspeed, the lift suddenly reduces to the extent that, perhaps, we can no longer defy gravity.

When flying at low level, these factors must be considered. The safe way to fly is to carry a safe airspeed margin above the stall and to keep the ASI in the pilot's primary scan:

attitude–airspeed–altitude–track

and

drift–attitude–airspeed–altitude etc.

What is Low Inertia?

You will hear the expression *low-inertia airplane*. This generally refers to a light aircraft with high drag. It has little momentum and resists any airspeed change. Thus it is safer in the trade-off between ground speed and airspeed. However, it is vulnerable in the case of engine failure at low speed. It will slow down and stall if the pilot does not dramatically lower the nose attitude to maintain flying speed.

Pilot Responsibilities

A pilot may not fly within 500 feet of any person, building, animal, etc., except when taking off or landing or in an emergency. There are other restrictions regarding flight over congested areas (1,000 feet above the highest obstacle) and large open-air gatherings (2,000 feet minimum lateral distance). Low cloud or some other unforeseen situation may force you below the minimum legal levels.

As a visual pilot, you are not qualified or trained to enter cloud; indeed, your aircraft may not be equipped for such flight conditions. If low cloud is encountered, it is better to fly slowly to give more reaction and decision time, but do not slow right down close to the stall. Lower part flap to improve the forward view and the margin over the stall. Maintain airspeed at the upper end of the flap-operating range (the white arc). Avoid cloud, scud, rain showers and high ground, and turn back as soon as possible.

Fly to one side of any valley to allow room to maneuver. Approach any high terrain at 45° rather than right angles so the turn away is easier. Cross the terrain only when you can see that the other side is clear.

Do not enter cloud or rain with high terrain ahead. Radio communications, which depend on line-of-sight transmission, may be poor.

It is far better to plan low flying rather than be forced to do it under adverse conditions.

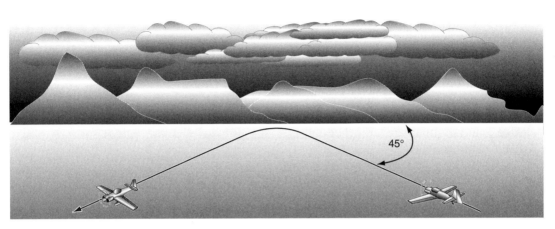

Figure 7-3. Approach hills at 45°.

Planning

Obstacle Clearance

A close study of charts of the area is advisable prior to flight, with special attention being given to the height of the ground above sea level, the nature of the terrain and the position of obstacles. Watch out for power lines and microwave towers. Take into account the wind direction and strength and areas of probable turbulence and downdrafts.

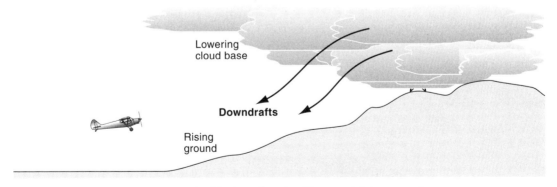

Figure 7-4. Avoid a lowering cloud base and rising ground.

At low level you have a limited field of view and limited visual range. At cruise speeds, surface features move rapidly. You need to anticipate any ground features and recognize them quickly. Low-level navigation is a special skill for which we all need specific training.

Judge your height above terrain visually, but keep an eye on airspeed and attitude.

Have the cockpit well organized and arrange your charts in a strip, aligned to your track, so you can hold it in one hand as you look ahead.

Aeronautical charts may not show spot heights below 500 feet MSL and obstacles below 360 feet AGL.

Some common-sense rules for obstacle clearance are:

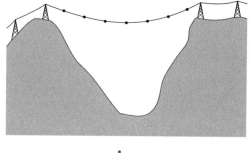

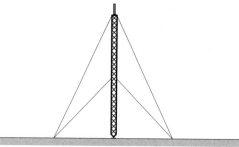

Figure 7-5. Elevated cables and the guy wires supporting transmission towers can be almost invisible.

- anticipate rising ground and climb early to maintain safe clearance;
- ensure that the airplane can actually out-climb the rising ground, especially if a wind is blowing down its slopes and you are low and on the leeward side or if you have a tail wind which will flatten the climb path (if in doubt about your climb performance turn away);
- avoid areas of rising ground under a lowering cloud base or rain showers
- until you are sure the other side is clear, approach rising terrain at an angle of 45° degrees rather than 90°, so that you have a shorter turn to safety; and
- always be prepared to turn back (decide early to turn back rather than continuing until you are forced to turn).

Ground Features

Features with vertical characteristics are good landmarks for low-level navigation. Hills, peaks, silos, towers, factory chimneys and radio or television masts fall into this category.

Figure 7-6. Choose landmarks visible at low level.

Effects of Atmospheric Disturbances

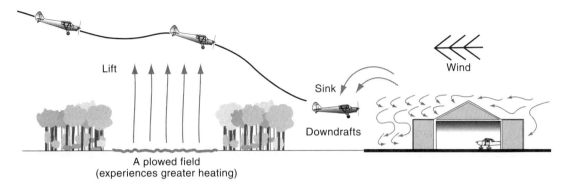

Figure 7-7. Atmospheric disturbances.

Wind

Wind is moving air. The aircraft is moving through a parcel of air. If the air itself is moving, then the path of the aircraft as perceived by someone on the ground will be a combination of the two motions (just like a boat crossing a river).

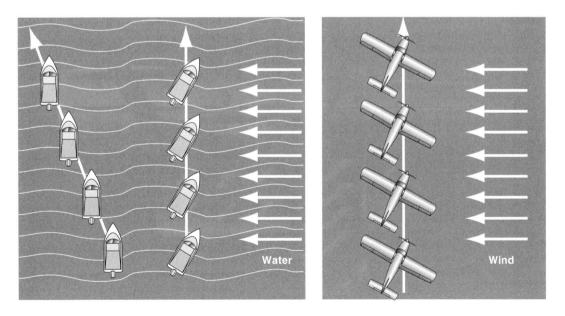

Figure 7-8. Heading (pointing) to achieve desired track (path).

Low Altitude

The effect of wind is more noticeable at lower altitudes where the relative movement of objects on the ground is more noticeable. If we are flying downwind, we zoom along; whereas into wind, everything seems slow which, relative to the earth, it is. But of course, we have exactly the same airspeed.

It is a little more complex when we are turning as both the ground speed is changing and so is the drift. If we are turning near the ground and we are looking at features, we seem to slide out of the turn (like skidding when we turn from downwind to crosswind, and we seem to drift into the turn when we turn from into wind to crosswind). Again all at the same airspeed and the aircraft is perfectly balanced.

Consider a weight swinging on the end of a string. The speed through the air is constant and equals the speed over the ground.

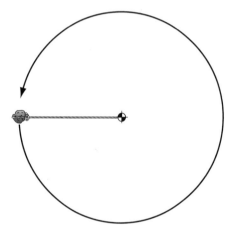

Figure 7-9. Center is stationary relative to the air.

Let's now swing the weight while on a moving platform. Standing on the platform, the weight would follow the circle as before being relative to the platform. If we were standing on a hill, looking down at the moving platform, we would see the weight following a spiral path.

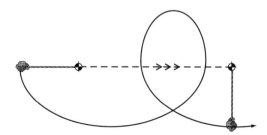

Figure 7-10. Center is moving relative to the ground.

If we now consider the aircraft flying a circle in a moving parcel of air, the effect is identical. From a balloon moving with the air, the aircraft would appear to follow a circle at a constant speed.

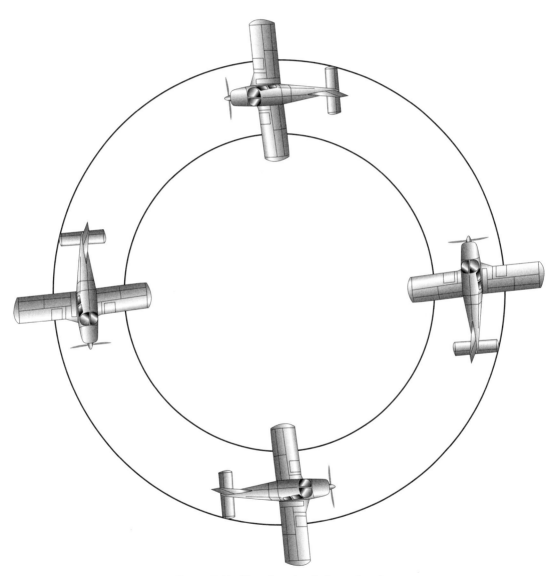

Figure 7-11. Aircraft path relative to the air.

But relative to the ground, the aircraft is changing from an into-wind path (no drift, slowest ground speed) to across the wind (maximum drift, ground speed equaling airspeed) to a downwind path (no drift, fastest ground speed) to another crosspath with drift now in the opposite direction.

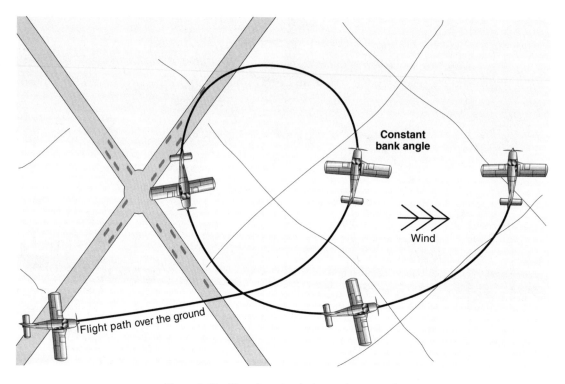

Figure 7-12. Aircraft path relative to the ground.

It can be a trap if the pilot tries to compensate for the apparent drift or speed by making control adjustments. The most dangerous is when going from the downwind path to a crosswind path and trying to stay within a feature on the ground. Air show pilots know this situation well. There is a great danger of an accelerated stall. There is a further danger if, on the downwind segment, the pilot feels too fast (which visual observation will confirm) and reduces power and airspeed when turning across the wind. This will further risk a stall. The pilot must cross-refer to airspeed and be sensitive to any excessive back pressure that may be wrongly applied. If in doubt, or uncomfortable, level the wings and climb.

Misleading Visual Effects

When flying at high levels, you are less aware of your passage over the ground, which may seem to be in slow motion. In low-level flight, however, both speed and drift are very obvious. The airplane flies in the air mass; its indicated airspeed has much more significance than its ground speed, and balanced flight is achieved when the ball is centered (even if the airplane appears to be slipping or skidding over the ground because of a crosswind).

A tail wind causes a false impression of high speed. An airplane flying with an airspeed of 70 knots in a 25-knot tailwind will have a ground speed of 95 knots. The nearness of the ground will give an impression of speed much greater than 70 knots, but you must resist any temptation to slow down. Reducing the ground speed to what feels like 70 knots would require an airspeed of 45 knots, which may be below the stalling speed. Check the airspeed on the ASI regularly.

In a head wind, the reverse is true. The ground speed is lower than the airspeed, giving an impression of low (rather than high) speed. Since there is no temptation to slow down, this situation is not as dangerous as the former one.

Sideways drift over the ground due to a crosswind causes false impressions of balance. In strong crosswinds, especially if the airspeed is low, the airplane will experience a large drift angle over the ground even though it is in balance. The false impression of slip or skid, especially when turning, can tempt an inexperienced pilot to use rudder to counteract it. This would place the airplane out of balance, degrade its performance and risk loss of control. Confirm balance with the balance ball. Since airspeed tends to fall in a turn, it is also good practice when flying low to have your hand on the throttle to catch the airspeed or rate of descent if necessary.

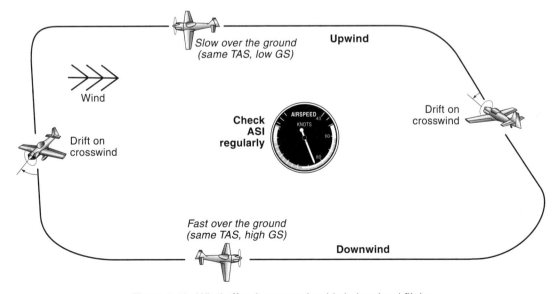

Figure 7-13. Wind effect is very noticeable in low-level flight.

Turbulence

Mechanical

Mechanical turbulence is caused by the wind blowing over, around, through and between various obstructions such as mountains, trees, buildings, valleys and tunnels.

The wind is forced up and slowed down as it approaches the object and can be severely disrupted causing eddy currents and vortices. The air is lifted over the object and then pours down and around the lee (downwind) side. There can be significant turbulence and downdrafts on the lee side of the hill and some smaller aircraft cannot climb as fast as the air is descending.

The stronger the wind, the greater the turbulence and the greater the danger. It is best to avoid hilly terrain altogether and especially, the lee side on a windy day. It is not very pleasant. In particular, stay away from cliffs, sheer faces, valleys, ravines and sudden changes in terrain.

Most of the severe turbulence is in the layers of air closest to the ground and the energy reduces as you get higher. One to two thousand feet of height above the local ground will clear you of the most severe mechanical turbulence—most of the time.

Thermals

Thermals are rising currents of air caused by the uneven heating of the ground. In summer, they can be quite severe and it is sometimes necessary to cruise at seven or eight thousand feet to avoid the worst turbulence. They are most severe if you fly under a developing or developed, lumpy, cumulus cloud. The thermal activity is strongest when the heating of the earth is most active. In summer, early mornings and evenings are a better time to fly.

When flying in turbulence, try to keep the attitude constant and ignore the pressure instruments—your control inputs may aggravate the situation. In a strong thermal, you may need to reduce power to maintain your selected altitude. Thermals also affect the final approach path.

Technique

Low-Flying Checks

Low flying is a higher risk operation. Prepare yourself and the airplane before descending.

- *Radio*—call before descending. Perhaps nominate a time for an OPS NORMAL call for search and rescue.
- *Harness*—make sure it is secure (there may be turbulence).
- *Mixture*—set to rich, unless over very high terrain. Carburetor heat perhaps.
- *Fuel*—check contents, selection, boost pump on. Note the time.
- *Instruments*—HI aligned. Altimeter set.
- *Wind*—note speed and direction and anticipate the effect of terrain.
- *Area*—orient yourself and the charts.

Aircraft Configuration

In good visibility, and over open country, the normal clean cruise configuration may be suitable for low-level flying. In poor visibility or in confined areas, where good maneuverability is required at reduced airspeed (to give more time to make decisions and take action), set the precautionary configuration with partial flap, and high propeller RPM.

The precautionary configuration allows:
- better forward view because of the lower nose attitude with flap extended;
- improved safety because of the reduced stalling speed and the greater time for the pilot to react or to make a decision;
- better maneuverability and smaller-radius turns because of the lower airspeed; and
- better response to elevator and rudder, due to the energized slipstream over the surfaces.

A disadvantage is the increased fuel consumption and the reduced range.

Technique

Vital points when flying low are:
- monitor the airspeed (resisting any temptation to slow down in a tail wind);
- keep in balance;
- stay well clear of obstacles and high terrain;
- avoid the leeward side of hills (downdrafts);
- avoid expected areas of turbulence (thermals and mechanical turbulence over hills); and
- keep a forced landing field in sight or in mind.

If you have to make a tight turn, apply full power and monitor attitude and airspeed in the turn.

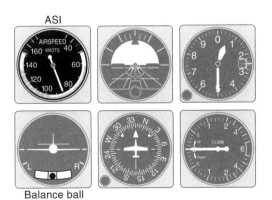

Figure 7-14. Monitor airspeed and balance when flying at low level *(altitude, instruments, attitude, lookout).*

Lookout

A good lookout is essential. Assess the area even before you commence the descent to low level to ensure that an adequate height above obstacles can be maintained and also look out for other aircraft. Beware of rising ground, especially if a wind is blowing down its slopes. Be careful if the horizon is poorly defined due to haze or drizzle.

Allow for Airplane Momentum

The airplane will take time to respond to any control movements due to its momentum (resistance to change of flight path). Commence climbs and turns early to avoid obstacles. Avoid harsh maneuvers (such as steep turns or high-G pull-ups) at low airspeed, which may lead to an accelerated (high-speed) stall. Reduce speed (or climb clear of the ground) if the turbulence becomes uncomfortable.

Trim

An airplane that is correctly trimmed is easier to fly and more likely to maintain altitude. Since your attention is directed out of the cockpit for most of the time in low-level flying, a well-trimmed airplane is essential.

Keep up the scan cycle of attitude–instruments–attitude–lookout (and position). If you prefer, a very slight nose-up trim will help ensure that an unintentional descent does not occur.

Bird Strike

The main decision with regard to a bird strike is to assess whether it has or will come through the windscreen, the engine/propeller or the flight controls, and what will be the consequences.

If you can avoid going under the bird, there is less likelihood of a strike. They tend to dive for the ground when they see or hear you, so try to go over them. If a bird is heading for your eyes, raise the nose and, if necessary, yaw the aircraft slightly to avoid a direct impact on the windscreen.

Do not do any air-show maneuvers or violent turns. Simply raise the nose and sideslip a little. If you have high power set and can temporarily do without it, then retard the throttle before the impact.

After any strike, check for damage and watch out for erroneous airspeed readings in case the pitot head has been damaged. Always set a combination of attitude and power that you know.

Fly home at a safe speed or, if in doubt about the serviceability of the airplane, land immediately and safely anywhere you can.

Let's now look at what it is like to fly some usual and not-so-usual taildraggers.

Part Three

Some Different Taildraggers

Introduction

This section of the book is included to allow pilots to share their experiences of flying some of the typical, and not-so-typical, taildraggers. Many of us fly ultralights, working airplanes, antiques and warbirds, as well as the regular tail wheel trainers such as Cubs and Maules. We can learn a lot from our professional colleagues.

Why?

It is all very well to study the theory of tail wheel operations—the dynamics and the options for control. It is also very valuable to hear what it is really like to encounter practical extremes of those same theoretical characteristics—the physically big, the multi-engine, the fast, the slow, the powerful, the heavy, the light, the under-powered and the delicate. There are wonderful lessons to be learned from hangar flying.

A parable is a story with a hidden or underlying message, as the following accounts certainly have. It is for us to learn from these and apply the lesson to our own flying techniques, building our pilot's toolkit of skill and knowledge.

Chapter 8

Austers

By Peter Whellum

General Description

(Note: These comments are based around the J/1B and J/1N, two popular Auster models.)

Austers are high-wing, single-engine monoplanes, with a fabric-covered, welded, steel-tube fuselage and a conventional landing gear. The fabric-covered wings, with a span of 36 feet, are constructed with wooden main and rear spars, and with aluminium ribs and leading edges. The tail assemblies are of tubular steel, also fabric-covered. Most Austers are fitted with the Gipsy Major, 130-hp, inverted, four-cylinder, in-line, air-cooled engine.

The Auster was developed by the Auster Aircraft Company of Great Britain as a military airborne observation post (AOP) aircraft. Their lineage can be traced back to the U.S. Taylorcraft, and are similar in appearance and performance to early model Piper Cub aircraft.

Austers served in uniform (camouflage) during World War II, mainly in the Pacific arena, as ambulance aircraft, artillery spotters and general runabouts for senior officers. Later versions were still in military service during the seventies.

Austers were used by the Royal Flying Doctor Service and charter companies, and were a common sight at many flying schools of that era. An Auster holds the dubious honor of being shot down off the coast of Sydney after becoming airborne without a pilot: the engine was hand-started with the throttle fully open and jumped the chocks. The aircraft took off by itself and there was a very real risk of it crashing into the densely populated suburbs.

There are many still flying even though production ceased in the late 1950s.

Flight Operations

Preflight

The preflight or daily inspection of any aircraft is a vital part of safety and should never be conducted in a rushed or hurried manner. Antique or historic aircraft should be treated in the same manner, but with even more care because of their age and usually different type of construction. With Austers, the following additional points are worth mentioning.

Always rotate the propeller through several turns (direction of rotation opposite to normal) to prevent a possible hydraulic lock inherent with inverted engines, with oil leaking past the cylinder rings and collecting in the cylinder head area. If not checked, serious damage to the engine is likely to occur when the engine is started.

Remove both left and right engine cowls to allow access to both sides of the engine bay where specific points—as mentioned in the pilot's operating handbook—should be carefully checked. Always exercise extreme caution when checking these areas. Do not forget to replace these cowls.

Chock the main wheels and, wherever possible, the hand-starting procedure should be a two-person operation.

Starting

Regardless of whether the engine is to be started by hand swinging or by an electric starter motor, it is always advisable to turn the engine by hand in the direction of rotation to shear the initial oil film, to avoid the risk of hydraulic lock damage and to draw a mixture of fuel and air into the cylinders.

Hand Swinging

Operate the priming levers on the left-side engine fuel pumps while pulling on the carburetor *tickler* control (float-depressing cable) until fuel flows from the induction manifold drainpipe. Wait for this fuel to stop draining before continuing.

Suck in by turning the propeller in the direction of rotation with the throttle closed. Switch on the battery master switch if applicable.

Open throttle slightly (about ¼ inch or so).

Switch on the starboard (right) magneto (the right magneto is equipped with an impulse mechanism that assists with hand-starting).

As soon as the engine starts, switch the left magneto on and set power to 1,000 RPM.

Taxiing

Because of the limited view over the nose during taxi, you need to adopt a zig-zagging taxi path to clear any blind spots immediately ahead of the aircraft. One of the more popular tail wheel assemblies fitted to Austers is the solid-rubber, Maule aircraft type which, although being steerable, becomes free castering when moved more than about 30° either side of center—very handy for manual ground handling. Steering is usually achieved via two spring-loaded control wires attached to either side of a control horn at the bottom of the rudder although its effectiveness is somewhat limited. When moving at low forward speeds, even full rudder may not apply sufficient force to turn the small tail wheel.

Takeoff

The crankshaft rotates in a counter-clockwise direction, which means the use of left rudder to counter swing during takeoff, left rudder during full-power climbs and right rudder during power-off (gliding) descents. At only 130 hp, the normal takeoff swings are relatively minor compared with higher-powered aircraft. Still, any yaw must be immediately corrected by left rudder to prevent a ground loop.

The faster you push the joystick forward to lift the tail during takeoff, the higher the gyroscopic forces and swing to the right; raise the tail smoothly and relatively slowly to minimize this effect.

While the extremely slow stall speed of 25 knots is handy for short takeoff and landing (STOL) performance, exercise extreme caution when you become airborne. Rotate between 35 to 40 knots (first stage of flap) and allow the aircraft to accelerate. Climb away at 55 to 60 knots. Retract the flaps at 200 feet.

The maximum-angle climb (45 knots) is steep.

Crosswind Takeoff

The Auster has a very low 8-knot crosswind limit. For the crosswind takeoff, apply into-wind aileron during the initial takeoff roll and delay your initial liftoff until 45 to 50 knots.

Climb out using the main (front) tank, choosing a cruise-climb airspeed between 65 to 70 knots, full throttle, with left rudder to balance the aircraft.

Always climb on full throttle. With the Gipsy Major engine, when the throttle is fully open, a cam on the throttle linkage activates a small push-valve on the carburetor, permitting a richer than normal fuel mixture into the inlet manifold. This ensures that sufficient fuel is available for not only for the full-power setting but also as an all-important cooling agent. Climbing at reduced throttle settings may cause damage by overheating the cylinder heads, which could lead to detonation and serious engine damage, not to mention reduced performance.

General Handling

During the cruise, elevator and rudder controls are quite sensitive, though aileron control is somewhat insensitive and a little sluggish. The overhead elevator trim control is very sensitive and only small inputs are required to affect any change in trim. The trim operates in a normal sense and hands-off flight is easy. The stall is easily controlled but the airplane will drop a wing if mishandled.

Descent

Spark plug fouling during descent is commonplace with inverted engines at the best of times, even with reasonable throttle settings. Application of carburetor heat during descent can minimize plug fouling, particularly when descending under reduced power, from high cruise altitudes, often regardless of weather conditions.

Bearing in mind the likelihood of plug fouling, experience has shown that descending with slightly less than normal cruise power results in a reasonably fast descent airspeed without too much danger of exceeding the generally accepted maneuvering speed of about 75 knots. Note that most Auster handling notes do not mention an official maneuver speed (V_A).

Approach and Landing (Three-Point Landing)

Turn onto the base leg at the normal position and reduce airspeed to 50–55 knots, which can be quite difficult, even with the throttle fully closed. If necessary adopt a high nose attitude to reduce speed. Passing through 57 knots, extend the first stage of flap.

During hot weather, particularly in the presence of thermal activity, it may be necessary to sideslip to reduce altitude to 600 feet AGL or so for the turn onto final approach. It is not unusual to have full flap selected with airspeed back to 50 knots and still be maintaining altitude; if so, you will need to sideslip, but be aware of the rapid rate of descent this configuration will cause. Always exercise caution with crossed controls at any altitude. Sideslip with flap extended is permitted.

Commence your turn onto final approach at about 600 feet AGL. Your target airspeed is 50 knots and extend the second stage of flap. Sideslip if necessary to achieve the desired approach path. Be aware of the high rate of descent and resultant inertia during the sideslip, particularly when close to the ground.

Do not forget the possibility of an over- or under-reading ASI during the sideslip due to the position of the static vent: usually over-reading for sideslip to the right (partially shielded static vent) and under-reading for sideslip to the left (increased airflow into the static vent).

Approach airspeed is 45 knots. Full flap (40°) can result in considerable drag. Correct any tendency to undershoot or overshoot by early use of power.

Do not leave the selection of full flap too late as any pitch change on short finals so close to the ground can be fraught with danger: the last thing you need is to be fumbling for the flaps and trim control when close to the ground. Having said that, try to trim the aircraft at all times.

Target threshold speed should be 30–35 knots with full flap—5 knots higher if only two stages of flap are being used. If your speed is any higher, you are likely to float a considerable distance before touchdown. After crossing the threshold, concentrate on the landing, look well ahead of your intended touchdown point and disregard the ASI. In any case, most ASIs fitted to Austers do not read lower than 30 knots and your airspeed should be just below this figure to commence the flare.

In strong wind, you may find that the ground speed during the flare is incredibly low and quite unsettling. This is normal for Austers. The aim is to stall the aircraft (at 25 knots) just above the runway and, if landing into a head wind of 15 knots or so, the ground speed will be 10 knots or less.

Where surface winds are 20 knots or more, the fun really starts with Austers! It can be quite an experience landing an aircraft that has zero or very little ground speed. In these cases you need to be careful judging your height above ground, moving your head quickly to use your forward, peripheral and even downward vision. Quite a challenge indeed when we have all been taught to look well ahead down the runway, and not at the runway beneath the aircraft!

Landing Roll

Once the aircraft touches down, close the throttle fully. Keep the joystick as far back as possible and apply opposite rudder at the very first sign of any yaw. At these low landing speeds, a ground loop can easily develop if not arrested early.

The rubber bungee cords used in the landing gear assembly have no damping effect and the stretched rubber will bounce you back into the air. If it does bounce, hold the joystick fully back, apply a little throttle and allow the aircraft to slow down and settle back onto the runway, closing the throttle when it does.

Keep the stick firmly back and apply sufficient power to arrest any increased rate of descent that may occur after bouncing. As soon as the aircraft has touched down again, immediately pull the throttle back, keeping the joystick fully back and maintaining directional control with rudder; apply into-wind aileron should any crosswind be present.

Stirring the Pudding

Many older pilots liken the sometimes fast and furious joystick and rudder inputs during the short final approach, flare, hold-off, touchdown and immediately after landing to *stirring the pudding.* You may well find that you require full rudder in either direction, as well as using the joystick, to control unwanted divergence from the runway centerline and to arrest any yawing of the tail or to correct any lifting or dropping wing. It can sound quite confusing, but it does fall into place. Like learning to fly formation, you eventually realize that most of the stirring is to counter your own overly excited control inputs and that the stirring serves no more purpose than to counter the stirring itself.

Summary

In a nutshell, Austers are one of the slowest-stalling, commercially built aircraft available, and that fact alone can be the cause of much excitement, intended or otherwise.

Cross-country flying in strong head wind and crosswind conditions can be extremely trying and tiring, with fuel or oil endurance being a major concern.

Many an Auster has been flown backward in demonstrations of their slow flying capabilities and, while fun to watch, the fun soon changes to trepidation when faced with extremes of head winds during a cross-country flight, particularly where fuel availability is in doubt.

Their extreme STOL performance can be both an advantage and a curse, particularly when operating from minimum-length strips with severe crosswind conditions. Their demands on the pilot are challenging but always satisfying. *Safe Austering.*

An Auster Anecdote by John Freeman

I was flying an Auster J/1N from England to the Sudan (south of Egypt) in 1957, prior to carrying out aerial spraying of cotton crops in the Sudan. I was in company with two aerial-spraying Tiger Moths. At airfields en route, I always waited for the Tigers to land.

Toward the latter stages of the trip, we arrived at Cairo International Airport. The main runway, which was some 10,000 feet long, was pretty well into the wind, and so we all flew a pattern to land on that runway. To avoid taxiing for long distances, we always aimed to land close to the far end of the runway adjacent to the terminal buildings.

The two Tigers landed and taxied clear of the runway to wait for me. I approached high and long, and flared 1,000 feet from the far end of the runway. It was a hot day and the Auster floated and floated and floated, until I was running out of runway. With much embarrassment, I decided to go around—much to the hilarity of the two pilots in the Tiger Moths. I believe that I may still hold the dubious honor of being the only light aircraft pilot to fail to complete a landing on Cairo's 10,000-foot runway due to inadequate length.

Chapter 9

Avions Mudry CAP 10B

By David Robson

General Description

The CAP 10B is a small, two-seat, fully aerobatic taildragger with side-by-side seating. It is made of wood, although a new version with a fiber-composite wing is now available. The fuselage is fabric-covered with a fiberglass upper deck. The wing is skinned with finely spliced plywood like a violin.

The design was developed from a home-built designed by Monsieur Claude Piel after World War II, which was inspired by the elliptical wing and elegant shape of the fabulous Spitfire. It was known as the *Piel Emeraude* (Emerald). As well as home-builts, many were manufactured in small batches.

The design was modified by Avions Mudry to meet a French Air Force requirement for a primary trainer, and it became the CAP 10B. Two significant changes were made:

- a change to plywood skins in place of the fabric covering on the wings to stiffen the wing and improve the roll rate (the previous fabric-covered wings would twist in response to aileron deflection—just like the F-86 at high speed—and would reduce the rate of roll); and
- a larger fin and rudder for positive spin entry and recovery.

(The aircraft were built with love. Monsieur Auguste Mudry, who was 77 years old when I visited his chateau some years ago, personally patted each aircraft under construction.)

The CAP 10B has been in production for more than 30 years without major design change—not bad for an operational military trainer! It has served with many air forces and became the basis for several successful competition aerobatic airplanes: the CAP 20, 21, 232, and 232EX.

The CAP 10B is powered by a fuel-injected, 200-hp AEIO-360 Lycoming with an inverted fuel system and Christen inverted oil system.

The landing gear is attached to the main spar of the wing and, unfortunately, landing with drift applied could damage the spar assembly and weaken the structure. Crosswind landings had to be made carefully to conserve the life of the structure.

The brakes are operated by small additional levers on the top outside of the rudder pedals. The pilot's feet need to be lifted to reach these pedals, and the outer part of the sole of the pilot's shoe positioned to operate the brakes. They are not very powerful and it is easy for the foot to slip off the lever.

The tail wheel is directly connected to the rudder steering via a spring-loaded detent. It pops out of the detent if steered tightly when the wheel would caster. It reseats when straightened.

Flight Operations

Starting

Engine start is routine for the fuel-injected engine, using the boost pump to build the fuel pressure. The stick is held back and the brakes positively depressed. The parking brake is released when the pedals are depressed, but you should not risk starting without your feet on the pedals. The early brake design allowed frequent leaks and air in the lines would sabotage the brakes. The brakes are independent and it is not unusual to lose one wheel brake on one side of the cockpit.

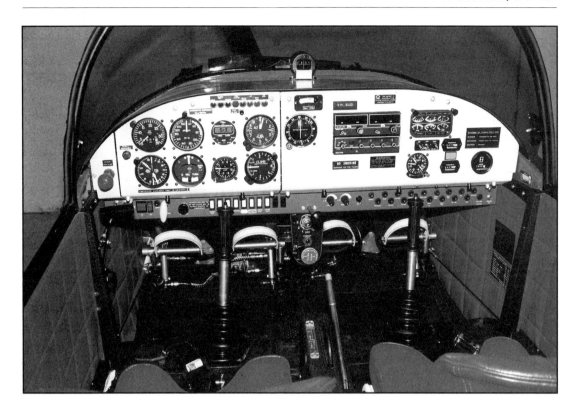

For example, one time on a check ride, the left brake failed as the engine started. The aircraft rolled forward and swung towards a fuel tanker as I stretched rapidly from the right seat to pull the mixture lever on the left side of the cockpit. My imagination went wild with visions of potential conflagration. The propeller stopped and the airplane stopped rolling just short of contact with the tanker. We stopped only just in time.

Taxiing

The view over the nose is quite good for a taildragger and steering is positive in winds up to 20 knots. Above this wind speed, it is difficult to taxi downwind and crosswind. The brakes are needed to assist steering and they will inevitably heat up and fade. The specified 20-knot crosswind limit for landing is in fact a practical taxiing limit.

Takeoff

The aircraft has positive control and accelerates quickly. Initial climb is steep and the field-of-view is spectacular. The bubble canopy gives a top-gun view. The pilot immediately feels as though it is a fighter plane being flown rather than a light aircraft. The controls are responsive. It will feel perfectly right from the start. This airplane is a natural extension of the pilot's hands.

General Handling

The CAP 10B has the nicest balanced control feel of any training airplane I have flown. There is little trim change with airspeed and power. The pilot can set the trim and power for high speed cruise and then complete a moderate aerobatic sequence without adjustment to either.

The fixed-pitch propeller does not overspeed if set to climb power and the airspeed is kept below V_{NO}.

The elliptical wing offers reduced induced drag at high angles of attack and so the aircraft can maneuver without loss of speed or altitude. It can actually climb through a moderate aerobatic sequence. It can be looped from level flight at normal cruise speed!

The CAP 10B has a good roll rate, but not spectacular when compared to its competitive sisters. It also has a cambered airfoil so almost full forward stick is required to hold a level inverted flight attitude.

It has a subtle aerodynamic buffet as the wing approaches the critical angle of attack—a good cue for maneuvering flight.

Approach and Landing

The flaps are manually operated by direct lever with a spring-loaded button. It is a little awkward to pull against the air loads and set full flap. The lever could slip from your hand.

The airplane likes an oval pattern—a constant turn from downwind to finals. The approach is easy to fly accurately, but airspeed has to be reduced early and full flap lowered. It does not have much drag from the flaps and, if you were high or fast, it is difficult to correct.

The pilot's feet need to be positively positioned on the brake levers for landing. It is too finicky to try this during the landing roll.

The CAP 10B may be landed either via a wheeler or a three-point landing, although it feels much more controlled on three points. It is much easier to land on grass and the flare can be so accurate that the wheels could brush against the blades of grass—a great feeling, much like a good golf strike.

As soon as on the ground, the pilot has to positively control direction and prevent any swing. There is plenty of control power, but it could quickly get away from you.

Summary

The CAP 10B is without doubt the most enjoyable light aircraft I have flown in more than 40 years of aviation. It is a true pilot's airplane. I love it.

Chapter 10

Austflight Drifter

By David Robson

General Description

The Drifter is a high-wing, ultralight, tandem, two-seat taildragger with a two-stroke Rotax engine driving a four-blade, Kevlar, pusher propeller. It is a fun airplane that requires good pilot skills to be flown accurately and well. It therefore has the attributes of a good training airplane, similar to the reputation of the famous Tiger Moth. The wings and horizontal stabilizer are fabric covered. It features full-span ailerons, and fabric elevators and rudder. It has conventional joysticks and the throttle is alongside the lower left rear side of the pilot's seat—a little awkward ergonomically.

The Drifter is a taildragger of a different ilk. It was originally designed in the U.S. and the license was bought to develop and manufacture the aircraft in Australia, hence it became the Austflight Drifter. It is manufactured at the airfield in Boonah, Queensland. It consists of a plastic chair balanced on a slender tube, which at several thousand feet above the ground feels very exposed. It has wings to wing, engine to thrust, and wheels to wheel. Everything is there to function. There are no luxuries, no redundancies. The pilot is there to pilot.

What good training it provides! It offers a valuable lesson in sideslip, yaw, rudder coordination, respect for wind, ground and air, threshold speed, anticipation, respect for the conditions, response to sudden engine failure, feel and sensitivity to changing airflow with airspeed, and awareness of wind shear. All in all, this airplane produces a more sensitive, aware and controlled pilot.

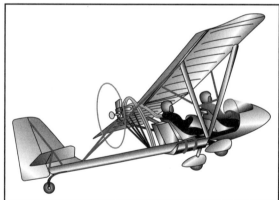

It offers a molded plastic seat (good ergonomics) supported by a couple of bolts into an aluminum tube (structural integrity) over an abyss of 3,000 feet of invisible air (aerodynamics). At 3,000 feet it feels a little (a lot!) insecure to look down alongside the fiberglass seat and see no visible means of support between your butt and the earth thousands of feet below. I dreaded looking down and had to force myself just to look at the horizon. Map reading takes some courage as it requires looking down. Drift is easy to assess: it is marked at such low airspeed, with the wind velocity a significant percentage of the resultant vector—whoever chose the name *Drifter* was a realist. The view is not only magnificent, it is a little alarming!

You sit *on* the Drifter, rather than *in* it. There is no inside. Everything is on the outside including the pilot. You are strapped to it—or it to you. The field-of-view is exceptional, if not extreme. The pilot is quite exposed, being suspended at the end of a pole projecting forward from the wing with his feet in a small plastic bucket. It feels like being the bait swaying temptingly on the end of a fishing pole, waiting for *Jaws* to rise up in front of you.

Flight Operations

Starting

The engine has an electric starter and the little two-stroke whirs into life, producing quite a different sound from a four-stroke. The throttle ergonomics are unusual. The throttle moves fore and aft for increase and decrease but, because the lever is at the base of the pilot's seat, the movement does not feel natural.

Taxiing

The Drifter has a steerable tail wheel assembly and taxiing is easy. It requires lots of RPM to move on rough ground or grass, but control is good, although the airplane is vulnerable to wind gusts. The brakes are quite effective. You feel like you are sitting in a model airplane, though. It's quite fun. In windy conditions, it is wise to have a human wing walker help steer and prevent the wing tip from lifting in gusts.

Takeoff

Even with two large pilots the little airplane shows good acceleration. It is easy to keep straight and the tail comes up easily. It has good directional control, from the energized airflow from the propeller over the rudder. The pilot needs to anticipate turbulence and downdrafts in the lee of trees and hangars. Both performance and pilot comfort depend on avoiding turbulence near the ground.

For liftoff, the pilot can rotate until the wheels leave the ground. But then what? How do you set the attitude with no structure in your field-of-view to set against the horizon? Amazingly, it is no problem. You are able to set the horizon *about there* and then correct for airspeed, just like you do in any airplane. The ability of human perception and skill to adapt and make do is surprising. The climb angle and rate is good.

Engine Failure

A heavy airplane with low drag will continue for a long time at speed. A heavy airplane with lots of drag will slow more quickly. Inertia or momentum is the tendency of the airplane to maintain flying speed after engine failure or in the presence of wind shear. A very light aircraft with very high drag will lose speed immediately, and only a major and sudden attitude change will allow gravity to prevent the deceleration. The Drifter has lots of drag and the nose must be lowered immediately to maintain flying speed. The nose does not drop by itself with engine failure. The pilot has to make a conscious control input to lower the nose quickly enough and dramatically enough to maintain flying speed. Like many ultralights, the Drifter also has pronounced adverse aileron yaw. Engine failure after takeoff in any ultralight is a seriously risky maneuver. It is fraught with danger if the pilot also tries to turn.

General Handling

The roll response is good with noticeable adverse yaw, but this is not a problem when the pilot uses appropriate (large) rudder inputs with aileron. In fact, it is a good training exercise for student pilots, even if they are to fly jets.

The pitch response is good with the following precaution: if you close the throttle suddenly the nose does not drop; it waffles as the airspeed reduces rapidly. This is the danger area after takeoff as mentioned. (The pilot would have to get the nose down a long way and do this quickly to hold gliding speed.)

The Drifter has an unbelievable field-of-view, to the point of making the pilot feel a little insecure. However, the control is good and the aircraft has the right feel. It is much like riding an aerial motorcycle and soon the sheer fun replaces any feeling of insecurity. It's a Harley with wings!

Stalling

The approach to the stall and the stall itself is conventional and predictable except there is not a powerful, nose-down pitching moment at the stall. The stall recovery requires a marked, positive, nose-down attitude change, which is a little alarming when the pilot first sees the earth three thousand feet ahead of the unobstructed view—*what am I doing up here*? (I tightened my harness, but suddenly found myself laughing aloud. I realized there was little point. I would only be firmly attached to an insecure airplane! The harness was not going to achieve much. What was the point?)

The aircraft or, more correctly, the airflow, provides a very clear sideslip indicator. The air enters the side of the pilot's helmet and visor, and twists the pilot's head if the aircraft is not kept in balance—providing another good training lesson.

Approach and Landing

The normal pattern is flown at 500 feet AGL. It can be positioned close enough to turn onto the final approach and land in the event of engine problems on downwind. Initially, aim for a touchdown point half way into the field, and then use sideslip to bring the touchdown back toward the threshold. The Drifter has no flaps so the pilot uses sideslip and slipping turns to lose altitude on the base leg and final approach to achieve a normal path to the threshold. There is adequate rudder power to achieve pronounced sideslips and the flight path control is easy. The attitude must be lowered, of course, to maintain airspeed. The roll rate is good with coordinated rudder input, even at pattern speeds.

Summary

The Drifter is the true motorcycle of the air. The pilot is exposed and becomes sensitive to all the elements of wind, turbulence and, especially, sideslip. The Drifter requires flying skill, judgment, anticipation and the active use of rudder.

Is it the ultimate basic trainer—the replacement for the Tiger Moth (Stearman) at long last? Perhaps it is. It is also great fun!

Chapter 11

Bellanca Citabria/Decathlon

By John Freeman
and David Robson

General Description

Citabria

The Citabria (*airbatic* spelled backward) was an aerobatic development of that long line of classic airplanes, the Aeronca Champion series. The Citabria offered a traditional touring design with the capability for some fun aerobatics. The original had a welded steel-tube fuselage with wooden wing spar and ribs. The whole airplane is fabric-covered. It has a fixed-pitch propeller, conventional flaps and toe brakes. Later the spar and ribs were fabricated from aluminum.

Decathlon/Super Decathlon

The Decathlon was a competition aerobatic airplane developed from the Citabria. It had a symmetrical airfoil, no dihedral, no flaps and a constant-speed propeller. Later, a higher-powered engine (180 hp) and an inverted fuel and oil system were added. This was the Super Decathlon. Later, modifications to the ailerons (spades) improved the roll rate to the extent that the Decathlon became a serious intermediate competitor.

The tail wheel is steered using the rudder pedals with a spring retention that allows catering for tight turns beyond the steering limit.

Flight Operations

General Description

The Bellanca Citabria 7GCBC is powered by a 150-hp Lycoming O-320 engine. It may be fitted with wooden or metal wing spars, and is fabric covered. Its seating is tandem, very comfortable and equipped with dual controls. It has toe-operated disk brakes to large or small wheels attached to leaf-spring landing gear. When equipped with large wheels (tires), the aircraft is a delight to operate on the ground, and rolls straight on takeoff or landing, demonstrating virtually no tendency to swing. The aircraft is flown solo only from the front seat due to CG constraints. It is equipped with simple flaps giving five settings from 7° to 35°. Flap recommendations are 7° or 16° for takeoff, depending upon takeoff distance available, and full flap for landing. Its maximum takeoff and landing weight is 1,428 lbs. It has a fuel capacity of 34.6 gallons contained in a tank in each wing root.

The left tank (17.8 gallons) is directly vented with a vent line across the top of the windscreen to the right tank (16.8 gallons). At times, this causes the left tank to exhaust its fuel while the right tank has a large quantity still in hand.

Starting

Starting is very simple using the Kigas primer for four strokes, switching both magnetos on, turning the master switch on, setting the throttle to ½ inch, and engaging the starter. Warm up at 800 RPM until the CHT gauge shows 212°F (100°C). Hot start is simply two primes with the throttle.

Taxiing

Taxiing is simple with good visibility from the front seat and very poor forward visibility from the rear seat when the front seat is occupied. The brakes and the steerable tail wheel make taxiing into a crosswind most comfortable, though downwind is also accomplished easily. In strong downwind situations, the control column should be held forward to depress the elevators and aileron should be raised on the opposite side to which the aircraft is to be turned, allowing the drag from the wind to help move that wing.

Takeoff

Takeoff is effected using either 7° or 16° flap setting, depending upon the takeoff distance available. Gradually opening the throttle to full power, there will be little, if any, swing, which is easily kept straight with rudder. Raise the tail to flying attitude and let the aircraft fly itself off. When clear of obstacles, position flaps up, reduce power to 2,400 RPM, and airspeed to 70 knots. The crosswind takeoff is easily effected by the upwind aileron being raised, keeping the aircraft straight with rudder and brake if necessary. The suggested maximum crosswind component is 10 knots.

Cruise

In cruise, power should be selected between 2,400 and 2,500 RPM, which should provide an indicated airspeed of 105 knots.

Approach and Landing

The approach airspeed is 60 to 65 knots, with 55 to 60 knots for a short final approach. The aircraft flares nicely. However, as full flap is 35°, the flaps will still produce lift and, therefore, there is a tendency for the aircraft to float. Should this continue, it is a simple matter to reach the flap handle, which is just below the throttle, and slowly raise the flaps that will then ease the aircraft onto the ground. Ensure the aircraft is at flaring height and three-point attitude before carrying this out.

Crosswind landings may be effected either using a wing-down basis or laying off drift and yawing straight as the aircraft settles. The upwind aileron should be raised until the aircraft has almost stopped.

Chapter 12

Cessna 185 Skywagon

By John Freeman

General Description

The Cessna 185 is a workhorse of an airplane with plenty of power and great lifting capacity.

It is powered by an engine of 260 hp or 300 hp. It has the traditional Cessna spring-steel conventional gear without damping (the airframe supplies aerodynamic damping, but only after the bounce). The tail wheel is steered via the rudder pedals. There is no tail wheel lock.

Flight Operations

Starting

The engine is started by turning on the fuel, selecting mixture to rich, setting full throttle and priming the engine with the electric fuel pump. Once primed, with the throttle set and a fine propeller pitch, operate the start key until all cylinders are firing. After start, turn off the electric fuel pump and warm the engine with between 800–1,000 RPM.

Taxiing

Experience in taxiing Tiger Moths is invaluable preparation for the 185 because, while it has brakes, it has many of the same problems, with its long fuselage and conventional gear. It wants to turn into the wind (weathercock) all the time. Taxiing into the wind is simple although, due to its high nose, clearing turns are recommended (swinging the nose left and right to see ahead). Ground control is easy with the steerable tail wheel and brake. The control column is held back when taxiing into and across the wind.

Crosswind taxiing may require application of opposite brake. Raising the upwind aileron is recommended. When taxiing downwind forward stick is applied to hold the tail on the ground. Raising the aileron of the wing, opposite to the direction of desired turn, helps to turn the aircraft (the drag produced by the tail wind on the upwardly deflected aileron assists the yawing moment). Reversing the aileron can help stop the turn.

Takeoff

The 185, particularly the 300-hp version, has a pronounced left swing on takeoff. Despite being a light aircraft, it demonstrates a swing on takeoff that is equivalent, in its own way, to a high-powered, piston-engine fighter plane (for example, the P-51). Consequently, it is imperative to start the takeoff roll with right rudder applied while holding the control column fully back. These control positions are maintained until some forward speed develops. Airflow over the keel surfaces is needed before trying to raise the tail, when the tendency to swing is most pronounced.

On takeoff, in the 185, there are only two places for the tail: either firmly on the ground or cleanly in the air with the airplane in the level attitude. The choice depends on airspeed and power, of course. The transition between the two positions is fraught and needs to be done with positive care. This airplane requires a firm hand and anticipation.

When liftoff speed is reached the aircraft will climb away very smartly. Flap is used for takeoff: 10° for a normal takeoff; and for a short field take-off, either 20° prior to application of power, or 10° initially increased to 20° just prior to liftoff. Once airborne, the flap should be slowly retracted when clear of obstacles. The manually operated flaps can be extended or retracted much more quickly than electric flaps. The movement needs to be firmly controlled.

General Handling

In the air, the 185 is a delight. Its control response is excellent in all three axes. The controls are relatively light and the aircraft is quite stable and easy to trim. It is fast: 300-hp models at 70% power true out at 147 knots at around 5,000 ft. Field of view is quite good with the usual wing-in-the-way problem of a high-wing configuration in the turn. The aircraft can be flown quite slowly—70 knots with 10° flap—for maneuvering and aerial observation. Its control response in this mode is excellent and its excess power provides rapid acceleration, if required.

Approach and Landing

View on final approach is excellent, particularly when 30° or 40° flap is selected. The aircraft is easily controlled and airspeed held steady with ample power to correct any undershoot. With full flap (40°) selected, 70 knots airspeed and the aircraft trimmed almost fully tail-heavy, it is easy to flare the aircraft into the correct three-point attitude for landing. Being a heavier aircraft than the Cessna 180, there is less probability of bounce if the above procedure is carried out. However, should the aircraft bounce markedly, it is recommended that power be applied for a go-around.

Crosswinds

Crosswind takeoffs must be carried out with care, particularly with left-side crosswind, which accentuates the swing due to torque, etc. Right-hand crosswinds can help cancel out the tendency to swing. At low speed and low power, the aircraft wants to wander to the right, particularly during the landing roll, even with a light left-hand crosswind.

Any tendency to swing left or right during the landing roll must be immediately counteracted as, once the swing develops, the forces created by the center of gravity being behind the wheels will overcome any force applied by rudder or brake to stop the swing. Should this happen, the aircraft will continue to swing uncontrollably off the airstrip and, if not able to slide sideways on wet ground, etc., the leading landing gear leg will collapse inwards, causing the wing and horizontal stabilizer to hit the ground. All of these damaging impacts are very expensive. (Swings of up to 110° from straight ahead have occurred.)

I know this from personal experience. When the airplane once swung to the right on landing, it became uncontrollable and deviated 110° from straight ahead. Fortunately, the aircraft ran onto barley grass and, while it still had a ground speed of some 30 knots, it slid sideways until it came to a halt with the wings rocking. I expected the landing gear to collapse and the wing to dig into the ground, but I was lucky. Except for both the student and myself uttering a very rude word when it swung, there was not much more to say. The lesson had been well learned.

Otherwise, it is recommended that, in crosswind conditions, wheeler landings are made to place the aircraft firmly upon its landing gear with the fin and rudder well exposed to the slipstream and the brakes having maximum effect with maximum weight upon the wheels. The tail should be held high as long as possible and then, without hesitation, lowered to the ground. As on takeoff, the only place for the tail to be is in the slipstream, in a level attitude, or on the ground. As with all aircraft, the aileron on the upwind wing should be raised until the aircraft has completely stopped.

Summary

The Cessna 185 is a high-performance single which, if flown correctly, can be an absolute delight. It is also an aircraft that, if you do not treat it with respect, may quickly show you that you have not learned it all yet. It may bite—either gently or severely!

Chapter 13

CAC CA-25
Winjeel (Little Eagle)

By David Robson

General Description

The Winjeel is a unique, Australian-designed, primary trainer. It is a low-wing, side-by-side trainer with an optional third crew position (rarely used for another pilot, but occasionally for a set of golf clubs).

The Winjeel was totally designed and manufactured in Australia to meet an Air Force specification for a basic training aircraft to replace the Wirraway (T-6), which was transferred from advanced to basic training after the phase-out of the Tiger Moth and the introduction of the Vampire as the advanced trainer.

The Winjeel is a low-wing aircraft powered by a supercharged 450-hp Pratt and Whitney radial engine (wonderful engine). It is large by civilian standards being a little smaller than the T-28 Trojan. It is fully aerobatic (but with a limited inverted time due to fuel and oil supply).

The pilots sit on seat-pack parachutes that fitted into a seat pan, like the World War II fighters, and they wear soft helmets with a separate outer shell.

The Winjeel has a tail wheel landing gear and was designed to depart from controlled flight at the stall and to autorotate if ailerons were used to pick up a down-going wing. This was a deliberate characteristic to teach the student a lesson; indeed, the fin was moved during development testing because it was difficult to cause it to spin since it was too directionally stable. (Unfortunately, this departure characteristic was to cost some lives when the aircraft was maneuvered at low altitudes in a role for which it was never designed and for which it was most unsuited: the FAC training role.)

It has right-hand sticks and left-hand throttle quadrants for both seats (beautiful). The control grips are the same as the F-86 Sabre and are beautiful to grip.

Landing Gear

The main wheels, fitted with low-pressure tires (so it can operate on soft grass), are carried on oleo-pneumatic struts that have a fairly short, stiff stroke. It is easy to bounce, but the most pronounced effect is caused by the tail dropping and the wing lifting the aircraft back into the air.

Tail Wheel

The tail wheel is selectable as either castering or steerable via the rudder pedals. There is a spring-loaded detent and pin which, when the control column was held hard back and the rudder bar wiggled left and right, will engage and the tail wheel then steers with the rudder.

To maneuver in a tight space, the control column is held hard forward and full rudder applied. The tail wheel will release and the aircraft spins around with the tail wheel castering. A touch of brake on the inner wheel will cause the airplane to turn on a dime. It is interesting to land after a lesson of spinning when full forward stick during spin recovery could have disengaged the tail wheel steering and the landing could result in a sudden departure!

Flight Operations

Starting

The big radial starts with a cough and puffs of blue smoke. There is always quite a strong smell of fuel or fumes in the cockpit.

After start, the big radial ticks over quietly and reliably. It makes a wonderful sound.

Taxiing

There is a reasonable view over the nose, and steering and braking are positive. It is easy to maneuver on the ground even in quite strong winds. The pilot must keep a firm grip on the column to prevent the control surfaces being blown about.

Takeoff

For takeoff, there is a detent on the throttle to avoid overboosting the engine. As the aircraft climbs, the gates could be passed to maintain sea-level boost up to full throttle height. There is a very convenient line of rivets along the side of the engine cowl. This not only gives a straight-line reference, but could also be used for pitch attitudes: climb (four rivets nose up), straight and level (two rivets nose up) and descent (no rivets). (Why don't all aircraft have rivets?)

General Handling

The controls are well balanced and the response is similar to the Chipmunk, being relatively light for such a large trainer. The roll rate is not spectacular and barrel rolls and slow rolls are difficult to perform well. In the looping plane, it is delightful and may be persuaded to complete a vertical eight if it was entered at V_{NE} and eased over the top of the top loop with a little takeoff flap. The torque of the engine makes stall turns very easy to the right, but difficult to the left.

There is a pronounced pitch and yaw with power changes, especially the nose-down pitching moment when the throttle is closed. This is worth remembering when considering the landing flare. It is wise not to close the throttle before the flare. There is also a noticeable nose-down pitch with large sideslip angles (large rudder deflection) due to shielding of the horizontal stabilizer and elevator.

The control response is generally good, with some adverse aileron yaw. A good pilot would need to keep the feet active to center the balance ball. It is argued that a good trainer is easy to fly, but difficult to fly well; this is exactly the case with the Winjeel. It was designed to depart from controlled flight at the point of stall, and so it punishes the cadet who tries to use aileron to pick up a dropping wing at the stall. It bites sharply. When turning steeply at low level, an experienced pilot carries a little top rudder so that, if the airplane departs, it rolls out of the turn and upward, rather than down into the turn and into the ground.

Approach and Landing

The Winjeel has three flap positions: takeoff, land and full. The split flap goes to 80° when flap was selected to full! The drag is high, the approach path is steep, and the approach speed is easily controlled.

The Winjeel is easy to land if the threshold speed is correct and if the throttle is not closed until after the flare was initiated. If too fast, the airplane has too much energy and wants to get back into the air. If the throttle is closed before the flare, the nose-down pitching moment is powerful and the probability of a soft touchdown is low. A wheeler requires a delicate touch and a positive forward pressure after touchdown. The wait while the tail comes down is fraught with expectation as the aircraft is vulnerable and departs sideways without any encouragement.

A three-point landing is the preferred technique and much more satisfying. There is sufficient elevator power to hold off until fully stalled. A smooth touchdown under these conditions is like hitting the sweet spot on a golf drive—magnificent.

Crosswind Landing

In a crosswind, the Winjeel is easier to land from a wings-level crabbed approach and a wheeler landing. The into-wind wing has to be kept down during the flare and the pilot has to actively stop any directional diversions. There is no room for relaxation.

Chapter 14

De Havilland Canada
DHC-1 Chipmunk

By David Robson

General Description

The Chipmunk was designed and developed by the Canadian company as a replacement aircraft for the British Tiger Moth. It became the standard military basic trainer for the Royal and Commonwealth Air Forces, cadet squadrons and air training corps for decades. It then followed the ex-military Tiger Moths into the aero clubs as the standard civilian trainer. Several were converted to specialized aerobatic mounts by some of the best display pilots in the U.S.

The Chipmunk accommodates two pilots in tandem, with the instructor in the rear. Both cockpits are covered with a single sliding canopy. The canopy may be partly opened in slow flight, but a cold climate, such as in England, is a deterrent to such fun.

The airplane is flown solo from the front seat (except for aerobatic competition airplanes). Both cockpits have joysticks rather than yokes. The Chipmunk is one of those aircraft that you feel a part of when you are strapped in; that is, you strap it on rather than merely sitting in it.

It is powered by a Gypsy Major engine, a 145-hp, four-cylinder, inverted, in-line engine that has a characteristic note and a significant oil consumption.

Flight Operations

Starting
The military Chipmunk has a cartridge start (a shotgun cartridge was fired by pulling a metal ring in the cockpit and the gas from the cartridge spun the engine to self-sustaining idle RPM). The civilian airplane has electric start. Both may also be handswung.

Taxiing
Steering and braking is unusual: the steering is by deflecting the rudder bar, with the degree of braking determined by the setting of a hand-brake lever that is set by the left hand. Full application gives parking brake on both wheels; half setting gives moderate braking on the side on which the rudder bar is pressed; the lever may be set to an appropriate level in between. It works well except that it momentarily takes the pilot's hand from the throttle. Murphy's law dictated that this occurred just when you needed to apply power.

The tail wheel casters throughout.

The view from the front cockpit is good and little deviation is needed to see ahead when taxiing. The front instrument panel feels closer than usual to the pilot's eyes.

Takeoff
The takeoff is routine: there is plenty of rudder power if the tail is left down until there is some forward airspeed. The aircraft swings right (not left). The tail comes up quickly and the rudder is effective as soon as power is applied and the slipstream energizes the rudder.

General Handling and Aerobatics
The Chipmunk is pleasant to fly, having a reasonable roll rate and light controls. The elevators are best, and this airplane loves the looping plane. The Chipmunk is capable of all basic, positive-G, aerobatic maneuvers. It is a delight for formation flying.

Loops are easy to fly, but rolls are more difficult. With no negative-G fuel or oil supply, the slow roll cannot be prolonged. The spin rate is rapid and almost full forward stick is required for recovery after several turns.

Approach and Landing
The Chipmunk naturally lands via a three-point landing, but may be landed as a wheeler due to the oleo-pneumatic landing gear legs that damped the touchdown.

The flaps are mechanically operated by a lever and detent. They are not powerful, but still useful.

Summary

The Chipmunk is one of the nicest taildraggers to fly, and one of the best in which to learn about flying. The aircraft is docile and fun.

Chapter 15

De Havilland DHA-3 Drover

By David Robson

General Description

The ugly/beautiful de Havilland Drover was developed for operations in the Australian outback for the Royal Flying Doctor Service (RFDS), specifically for short sectors and rough-field operations. It is a unique Australian-designed aircraft with some structural features from the wing center-section design of the British de Havilland Dove (a twin-engine, tricycle-gear airplane of similar size). The Drover was designed immediately following World War II, and was originally conceived as a twin-engine aircraft.

Due to war priorities, there was no readily available civilian engine with enough power so the design was changed to accommodate three lower-powered engines. Production versions of the Drover are powered by three Gypsy Major engines (the Drover was once described as three Tiger Moths in close formation). They consume their oil capacity in about the same time as they consume the fuel capacity. We used to carry several (a dozen or so) cans of oil on any cross-country trip.

The Drover has fixed-pitch propellers, fixed gear, three engines and one pilot (the perfect ratio?). It has hand-pumped hydraulic flaps, a beautifully soft, long-stroke landing gear, and gentle, docile flight characteristics. However, it is also slow and uneconomical. It suffered the fate of a poor bottom-line since it was not as profitable as other types.

In all, though, it was loved by outback pilots who even wrote a song to the Drover: *I'm looking over a four-leaf clover* becoming *I'm looking over the nose of a Drover.*

Antique airplanes, as Drovers are now, have a characteristic smell: a mixture of leather, oil, petrol, sweat and, perhaps, fear. Whenever I walk out to the Drover, open the door and attach the step ladder, it reminds me of Bogie and Bergman saying farewell in *Casablanca.* (Hopeless romantics, we pilots. *Play it again, Sham.*)

Flight Operations

Engine Start/Priming

The prestart sequence is a powered equivalent of the hand-swinging technique for the same engine in the Tiger Moth. Set mixture to rich, prime the right engine first (because of the left-side passenger door), select the fuel pump on for 8–10 seconds or until the ground crew says that fuel is dripping from exhaust, then the sequence is pump off, throttle open, switches off, crank for three seconds, throttle set, switches on, and start.

Taxiing

The Drover has the same hand-lever/rudder-bar braking system as the de Havilland Chipmunk. The degree of braking is set by a lever like the handbrake lever of an antique car. If the brake is fully applied, both brakes are hard on, and therefore parked. If the lever is fully released, there is no braking, just rudder steering. If the lever is set somewhere in between, the deflection of the rudder bar also applies some braking to one wheel. Therefore, the aircraft is steered with rudder and castering tail wheel and, to tighten the turn, the inner wheel is made to *bite* with the application of some handbrake. For straight-line taxiing, only a little brake is set and it is only operated with large rudder deflections. On the whole, it is a good system, but occasionally the left hand becomes occupied so the right hand has to be placed across your lap to operate the throttles, which therefore means the control column must be held back with the knees and right elbow while the feet are trying to steer. It is a little like pedaling a bicycle, rubbing your belly and pumping for spring water, all at the same time!

Differential power is a subtle and useful means of control in a crosswind and during the early stages of the takeoff roll. It is also useful for tight maneuvering with brakes. This airplane can be turned on a dime.

Takeoff

The flaps are operated by setting a lever and then pumping a mechanical/hydraulic hand-pump with the right hand. It is quite hectic after takeoff on a gusty day to let go of the throttles, change hands and pump the flaps up. I believe the Spitfire had a similar system for the landing gear.

Takeoff is short and the acceleration good. When it is ready the aircraft lifts off and climbs steeply without changing attitude. It goes up like the elevator in a skyscraper.

It is impossible to have all three engines in sync for more than a second on takeoff, so the droning must be accepted until steady in the climb.

General Handling

The Drover is easy and pleasant to fly and full of character. The forward view is good and the cockpit roomy. The big windows give the passengers an excellent view. Control forces are light, but the roll rate is slow. It is a continual task to keep the engines in sync.

Despite the high aspect ratio and low wing loading, the Drover rides the wind well. Turbulence provides little concern.

One has to plan well for longer trips, though. The Gypsies burn oil as quickly as they burn fuel, making frequent stops and many cans of oil necessary.

Approach and Landing

Normal landing for the Drover is a tail-down wheeler to give better control of the touchdown, and to maintain flying speed and good lateral control. (The wing likes to lift with the wind.)

Threshold speed should not be too slow as the elevators lose the power to control the touchdown. Nor should it be too fast as, in ground effect, it does not want to stop flying: it just continues to float.

The incredibly soft, well-damped, long-stroke landing gear makes up for any pilot inaccuracies on touchdown. An average landing in any other airplane would become a greaser in the Drover as the landing gear helps the pilot to land.

The double-slotted flaps give a low threshold speed and so a very short landing.

Braking is good even if the tail is up. The Drover is a good short-field airplane.

Crosswind

There is no strong yawing tendency with a crosswind; rather, the into-wind wing would gently and gracefully lift and the pilot had to be quick and forceful to keep it down. It will gracefully drift you off the side of the runway if you are not careful.

Summary

The old Drover is probably the easiest taildragger, and the most pleasant vintage airplane, I have flown; nevertheless, it would gently carry you off the runway if you were not positively in control. Fly it again, Sam?

Chapter 16

De Havilland D.H.82
Tiger Moth

By John Freeman

General Description

The Tiger Moth was the natural evolution of the Moth series of biplanes, having staggered wings and a swept upper wing (mainplane) to improve the pilot's view. It became the standard training aircraft for the Royal Air Force and the Commonwealth air forces of Australia, Canada and South Africa.

The actual birth of the D.H.82 Tiger Moth is, in itself, a great story. The Air Ministry in England put out a specification for an ab initio trainer for the RAF. One major point was that it should seat both instructor and student wearing seat parachutes. The existing D.H.60 Moth fitted the bill pretty well, except that in the D.H.60 it was not possible for the instructor to climb into, or more importantly, out of the front cockpit wearing a parachute because the fuel tank in the top mainplane got in the way. The D.H.60 wings were not staggered, being aligned above each other. One evening at the de Havilland works at Stag Lane, North London, the engineers set about overcoming this problem. They unbolted the top mainplane, fuel tank and center section and moved them forward to a point where entry to and egress from the front cockpit was possible. This, of course, moved the center of gravity forward so they then swept the wings back to overcome this. Now they had the bottom wing tips too close to the ground so they lifted the bottom wing tips to give clearance and so dihedral was added. Finally, they bolted it all together and flew it. All without drawings, they had produced one of the finest basic biplane trainers the world has seen.

Thousands were built for the massive training effort needed during the World War II. The Tiger Moth was the anglican equivalent to the Stearman. At the end of the war many were made available for private use. They could be bought for a few hundred dollars in brand new condition.

Many adopted the Tiger as the standard trainer. Some were converted for agricultural use. It is powered by a four-cylinder, inverted, 130-hp Gipsy Major engine with a two-blade, fixed-pitch propeller.

Intercockpit communications were via a Gosport tube, which worked brilliantly; indeed, better than the average intercom I have found on so-called modern aircraft. The Gosport tube was simply a speaking funnel that carried sound waves via rubber hoses from one pilot's mouthpiece to the other's ear-pieces—like the old switchboard operators speaking tubes (and not unlike two tin cans and a piece of string).

The Tiger Moth was considered the perfect trainer as it was easy to fly safely but difficult to fly well—or so they said. It certainly taught the student pilots to use their feet, to respect wind, to achieve the right threshold speed and to look for forced-landing areas (continuously).

It had no wheel brakes, and a tail skid rather than a wheel. However, later modifications to allow operations from sealed strips included brakes, tail wheel, electronics and a radio (sacrilege).

A total number of 8,811 Tiger Moths were constructed.

Flight Operations

Starting

The traditional Tiger Moth does not have an electric starter; engine start is by hand-swinging the propeller. It is a two-person operation, involving both the pilot and the starter. The hand swinging, in itself, takes some skill, training and caution. (Do not wear a neck-tie or loose clothing.)

The nose is high in the air, and care must be taken to position the propeller and then to allow the pilot to activate the magnetos before swinging the propeller.

If you are the starter, always have someone in the cockpit who knows what they are doing.

The magneto switches are individual, paired, two-way switches, externally mounted on the upper left side of the fuselage, ahead of each cockpit. The right magneto (the forward switch of each pair of switches) has slightly retarded timing, and so is used alone for starting. After start, the left magneto is armed.

The pilot in the rear cockpit looks after the throttle and rear set of magneto switches. The front-seat pilot, or the person swinging the propeller, looks after the front set.

If you are the starter, the last thing you want to do is to overprime or underprime the engine. You could be there for a long time. The mixture (correct priming) is vital. It deliberately floods the engine then evacuates excess fuel and sets the ideal mixture for each and every start. It works reliably.

The calls are very important. Many a close shave has occurred, or an aircraft has jumped the chocks, resulting in exclamations such as, *I thought the switches were off!* or *You said the throttle was closed!* This time-honored ritual, learned by hard experience, is described below.

Technique for Hand-Swinging the Propeller

(Do not attempt it without hands-on instruction.)

Priming is carried out with fuel on and jiggling the brass knob on the carburetor top until fuel trickles out of the overflow pipe underneath the engine. In very cold weather, this pipe can become blocked with oil, making starting impossible, and therefore it needs cleaning to get overflow and a proper prime.

After priming the carburetor, check both sets of magneto switches off and the throttle is closed.

The starter calls, "switches off, throttle closed."

Both pilots (or pilot and starter) should check their magneto set. The pilot calls back, "switches off, throttle closed".

The starter sucks fuel–air mixture into the engine by rotating the propeller clockwise through four compressions. The starter calls, "switches off, throttle open."

With the magnetos still off, the pilot opens the throttle fully and calls, "switches off, throttle open."

The starter evacuates the cylinders by pulling the propeller counter-clockwise through eleven times (counts eleven blades).

The starter then calls, "switches off, throttle closed."

The pilot closes the throttle and reads back the call.

Now, with the throttle closed, the starter sucks in fuel by one blade rotation clockwise. The starter places both of the forward pair of magneto switches on, then pulls the propeller so it is set just before compression and about the two o'clock position. (Remember the propeller rotates clockwise as you see it when standing in front.)

The starter should confirm chocks are in and call, "switches on, throttle set, contact!"

The pilot turns on the front magneto switch of the pair, sets the throttle ½ inch open and holds the stick fully back (the brakes and parking brake are also applied if the aircraft has either or both). The pilot then calls back, "switches on, throttle set, contact!"

The starter swings the propeller clockwise with a firm but smooth flowing pull through, continuing to turn so that the arms are clear of the propeller arc. (Be careful not to lean or bend forward as you pull—do not look down as your hands drop.) The swing is a turning motion of the body similar to a golf swing. The pull does not have to be violent. The engine only has to go through one compression for the magneto to fire the spark plug. If the mixture is right, it will start right away.

Swinging should be done by reaching two inches from the top of the upper part of the propeller and pulling it through its compression while swinging the body clear. Some starters place their right hand on the prop blade and hold their right wrist with their left hand. This combines the swinging power of both hands and ensures that both clear the propeller arc as they pull through.

Alternatively, starting can be done from behind the propeller. This is safer as you can swing single-handed and hold the center section strut with the other hand. It is also easier to reach the front magneto switches if it is necessary to cut the ignition.

If the engine does not fire, the starter calls, "switches off, throttle closed."

The pilot responds.

The starter sets the propeller at two o'clock and calls, "switches on, throttle set, contact!" and tries again.

If still no start, and there is a smell of excess fuel, the engine has been overprimed and should be evacuated by rotating the propeller backward ("switches off, throttle open"). Otherwise, reprime and go through the whole process again.

The Tiger Moth engine has two magnetos, with only the right one being an impulse magneto. This is on the starboard side of the engine. If, on swinging the propeller clockwise, no sound of impulse is heard (that is, no click of the contact breakers), you should tap the rear of the magneto to free the impulse mechanism. The manufacturer recommended using a two-shilling piece, but practice showed that a firm thump with a heavy screwdriver or wrench did the trick, as indentations on all Tiger magneto covers attest.

After start, the pilot places both magneto switches on, checks the oil pressure and warms engine at 800 RPM. After about four minutes of warm-up, the engine is run up to full power (2,000 RPM), and each magneto switched off, in turn, to check maximum RPM drop of 150.

Then the chocks are waved away for taxiing (throttle set to idle until the starter is clear).

Taxiing

If the aircraft has wheel brakes and a tail wheel, it is steered like any other taildragger.

Taxiing an original Tiger Moth with the tail skid is an artform due to the lack of brakes and its sensitivity to wind gusts. The tail skid is moved side-to-side by two small horns on the bottom of the rudder that bear against the tail skid spring, and so give tail skid steering.

It works beautifully on grass since the drag keeps the aircraft straight and skids the tail around when deflected to turn. The aileron can vary the weight on each main wheel thus increasing the friction, on that side, considerably. On grass, and in light winds, the aircraft can be gently steered simply by applying aileron in the desired direction of turn.

If the ground is hard, such as on concrete, the skid does not bite into the surface and so steering is lost. (The ailerons are still effective for gentle turns.) In countries where the summer surface is hard, welding a small piece of a steel file on edge on the bottom of the tail-skid spade solves the problem it provides a hard edge to bite into the harder surface like ice skates. However, on these surfaces only gentle turns should be made, allowing plenty of room. It is far better to find a wing walker to pull on one wing tip, or even to lift the tail and carry it around, to help you pivot around in a tight space. As much as possible avoid taxiing the aircraft on bitumen or concrete surfaces.

Taxiing into wind is relatively simple as the large rudder acts in the slipstream to help steer the aircraft. Holding the stick firmly back increases the friction of the skid and helps steering. Taxiing crosswind is difficult as the aircraft wants to weathercock and the upwind wing wants to rise. Holding the control column into the wind (the upwind aileron is raised) helps to some degree, but the only easy way is having a person hold the upwind wing tip. Ideally, have a person on each wing tip (wing walkers).

Taxiing downwind can be most frustrating because the aircraft wants to weathercock back into wind. Lifting the aileron on the side opposite to the direction of turn helps because the drag from the reverse flow over the raised aileron counters the weathercocking.

When taxiing downwind the stick should be held forward so the reverse airflow, over the large elevators and stabilizer, holds the tail on the ground. Again, manual assistance on the wing tips is best. At all times, taxiing speed should not exceed a fast walking pace. When things go wrong, they go wrong quickly and, the faster one taxies, the more likelihood there is of tipping the aircraft onto its wing tip or nose, or of hitting an obstacle.

Takeoff

Taking off into the wind is relatively simple provided that one does not raise the tail too quickly. The Tiger's elevators are powerful and can almost raise the tail when stationary. So, stick back until there is some forward speed and good airflow over the tail surfaces, then raise the tail when the rudder is effective.

Raising the tail before some forward speed is established can result in the corkscrew effects of the engine (slipstream, torque reaction and gyroscopic effects) causing the aircraft to swings to the right before the rudder has enough power to counter the swing. Remember that you have no brakes!

Engine Failure

A heavy airplane with low drag will continue for a long time at speed. A heavy airplane with lots of drag will slow more quickly.

Inertia or momentum is the tendency of the airplane to maintain flying speed after engine failure or in the presence of wind shear. A very light aircraft with very high drag will lose speed immediately, and only a major and sudden attitude change will allow gravity to prevent the deceleration.

The Tiger Moth has lots of drag and the nose must be lowered immediately to maintain flying speed. It also has pronounced adverse aileron yaw and a tendency to drop a wing at the stall. Engine failure after takeoff in the Tiger is a seriously risky maneuver, especially if the pilot also tries to turn back.

Crosswind Takeoff

Maximum crosswind component for the D.H.82 is 7 mph from the left and 12 mph from the right. This with stick held firmly back until good airflow is established. Raising the tail too soon will result in diversion to the right even with a left-hand crosswind due to the corkscrew effect. Raised aileron on the upwind side is essential.

General Handling

In the air, the Tiger is a delight with nicely balanced controls. The rudder is heavy due to its size and small balancing area, but it is very powerful. The elevator and aileron forces are light. The ailerons are differential, which reduces adverse aileron yaw. However, the rate of roll is not fast. Ailerons are fitted only to the lower mainplanes. Aerobatic rolling maneuvers are therefore quite difficult.

During a slow roll or barrel roll, it is easy to run out of aileron power as the airspeed slows through the inverted attitude. You are then stuck upside down with the engine coughing and the nose dropping. Rudder and elevators are powerful and loops, stall turns and recovery from spinning. The high-lift wings, enormous wing area and low wing loading make looping maneuvers very tight, although the enormous drag requires a steep entry to build sufficient energy to be able to complete a loop. The pilot places the aircraft in an attitude where, from the rear cockpit, the upper mainplane is on the horizon; that is, the airplane is in an attitude of about 45° nose-down!

The open cockpit combined with the small windscreen means that there is plenty of wind on the face to help indicate slipping or skidding. It is truly an aerial motorcycle. In areas where there are large insects or it is cold, a handkerchief worn between the goggles and the helmet chinstrap can save one's lower face from damage. The same applies in hot weather due to potential sunburn and windburn. The problem is not so great in the front cockpit as the upper wing provides shade.

The engine seemed to burn as much oil as fuel, and it is usual to end up with your face and goggles covered in a thin film of oil. Now you know why World War I pilots wore scarves.

Approach and Landing

The view from the rear cockpit is somewhat restricted and, combined with absence of flaps, increases the possibility of overshoot. Both these problems can be overcome in sideslip, which is easily carried out in the Tiger (and is quite delightful with the wind on one's face). The powerful rudder allows very steep, controlled descents while side-slipping. If correct airspeed is maintained, the sideslip is easily controlled and can be steepened or made shallower with more or less application of rudder and opposite aileron. Recovery is quite straightforward to the glide.

The glide approach is standard and the pattern is flown so that the aircraft can reach the field after an engine failure at any stage. The engine is generally reliable, but it is not like modern engines.

The usual approach speed for the Tiger Moth is 59 knots (65 mph) and, if this is selected and maintained with full tail-heavy trim, the aircraft is easy to flare, float a little and arrive on three points. The three-point arrival is recommended due to its lower speed. Despite the long nose, it is easier to judge the flare from the rear cockpit than from the front. The long nose is a good reference for attitude and direction, and peripheral vision should be trusted.

Tail-up, wheeler landings should be approached with caution as the aircraft (having no brakes) is difficult to keep straight when the tail is lowered out of the slipstream and before the tail skid touches the ground.

Glide approaches are best, so you should stay within gliding distance to the field.

One last point: care must be taken not to hold off bank (lowered aileron on the lower wing) in gliding turns. If the airspeed gets slow, the lower wing has a greater angle of attack because of the down aileron. The high-side wings are still generating lift. The airplane can easily auto-rotate and spin. As the aces used to sing, "we watched him sizzle, we watched him burn, he held off bank in a gliding turn."

Crosswind Landings

Crosswind landings must be approached with great caution. The wing-down method is the only way with the wing held down right through to touch down. Once on the ground the aircraft can be allowed to weathercock into wind as it slows.

The adage *if the crosswind is over five knots, go somewhere where you can land into the wind* applies to Tiger Moths.

Summary

In summary, the Tiger Moth is slow, has a poor rate of climb, is cold in winter, hot in summer, has little range and is not a particularly good aerobatic machine. However, it is a safe, strong aircraft and a delight to fly for fun.

Some Life Lessons For the Tiger Moth Pilot

Taxiing

There was a time-proven (but highly illegal) method of taxiing a Tiger on bitumen, concrete or very hard ground, with no help at the wing tips. Provided it was not at a controlled airfield, the pilot would get out of the cockpit and walk alongside the airplane, holding the throttle and using just enough power for a slow walk. The rear fuselage could be pushed and pulled sideways to ensure that the aircraft went where needed. Don't trip though!

Starting When No Help Is Available

Some pilots (foolishly) have tried to hand-start the Tiger without assistance. Some aircraft have ended on their noses. Some have collided with others. Some have even taken off and had to be avoided or even escorted until they ran out of fuel and crashed.

In the late 1950s, I left a commercial pilot, who was working for the company as an organizer, at Kidlington Airport in Oxford, England. Gaining experience, he was to ferry my aerial spraying Tiger to the working airstrip. He was to have arrived by the time we arrived by road, but did not. Some 20 minutes late, he landed looking a little pale. I asked whether he have a problem, to which he replied no.

Later, on a subsequent visit to Kidlington, I found out what had happened. He had pushed the Tiger out of the hangar and left it some distance out but pointing toward the hangar. He then proceeded to start it without using wheel chocks. However, he did not close the throttle after the blow out sequence and consequently when he swung the propeller to start the engine, it started at full power! The aircraft moved forward. Fortunately, he had swung the propeller from the rear and so was not in the way of the propeller.

Agricultural Tigers in the U.K. had their rear magneto switches on the instrument panel, above the compass. Forgetting the front magneto switches on the fuselage, he tried to climb over the wing root to get to the magneto switches in the rear cockpit. Unfortunately, as he stepped upon the wheel to do this (it was rolling), he tripped over the flying wires and fell head-first into the rear cockpit. The engineers in the hangar heard the roar of the engine and rushed out to see the Tiger moving rapidly toward the hangar with a pair of legs sticking vertically out of the rear cockpit. The pilot managed to reach up and switch off the magnetos and the engine stopped, as did the Tiger before hitting anything. The engineers then went to the aircraft, lifted out the pilot, put him back into the cockpit the right way up and restarted the engine. He then left red-faced and contrite.

Crosswinds

I was flying a Tiger on crop-spraying operations. Takeoff was heavy and landings light and frequent. The crosswind was just okay for takeoff. But this was a one-way agricultural strip and the crosswind was excessive for landing. It was most frustrating, until I decided to try landing across the strip into the wind. It worked and so, for the next 20 trips, I did this until the wind became too strong for the heavyweight crosswind takeoff. The strip was 213 feet wide. Day after day, with a takeoff and landing every five minutes, sometimes 100 flights in a day, this produced an amazing degree of confidence and level of flying skill.

Aerobatics

Practicing a slow roll over a small group of houses one day, I ran out of aileron and got stuck on my back. Just before recovering by means of a half loop out of the bottom, the cockpit fire extinguisher came loose and fell out of the aircraft, clipping me on the chin on the way. It then disappeared down toward the houses. In a blue funk, I scuttled back to the airfield, landed, taxied in and sat awaiting the telephone call to say that I had bombed someone. Happily it never came.

Securing the Aircraft

It is most important to tie down an aircraft even if away for a short period. This particularly applies to Tiger Moths.

A pilot left a Tiger unsecured on a bitumen runway, part of an old wartime airfield in England. The aircraft was not unattended for long—just time enough to get some sandwiches—but long enough for a strong gust of wind to pick the Tiger up and position it neatly inverted on the fence with the fence posts poking through the wings.

There are also tales of Tigers being landed in fields and the fabric being eaten off the wings by cattle. They love the flavor of the dope.

Crosswind (Again)

While carrying out aerial top-dressing operations from an airstrip right on the coast that had a lateral slope left down to right, as well as a light crosswind from the left, I was surprised to find the aircraft swinging right causing me to run off downhill dumping the payload as fast as I could before slipping over the edge of the cliff and out to sea. An older, wiser agricultural pilot was operating another Tiger Moth, and after witnessing this, got out of his aircraft to suggest that I keep the tail on the ground until I had good airflow over the keel surfaces, even explaining to me why. By doing this, I had no further frights.

Chapter 17

Douglas DC-3 (Dakota)

By Captain Don Hutchison

General Description

The famous Douglas DC-3 was one of the pioneer all-metal airliners used extensively by both civil and military customers. It is arguably the most significant and longest serving aircraft in civil aviation history—the grand lady of the skies.

It is powered by two Pratt & Whitney, twin-row, Wasp, radial engines each of 1,200 hp. A crew of up to four may be carried (typically, two pilots and a navigator, and sometimes a radio operator).

A massive number of the military version, the C-47, have served all over the world, and many are still in service. The Royal Australian Air Force only retired its last aircraft in 1999. There has been much talk of a Dakota replacement, but it is so unique that I do not believe it will ever truly be replaced by a single aircraft type.

Flight Operations

I first flew a DC-3 in 1964 as a first officer for Ansett Airlines of Australia. After endorsement training in Melbourne, I transferred to a tight-knit group of a dozen or so pilots, based in the city of Cairns in far North Queensland. Our main task was to service the community in the Cape York peninsula area, with daily passenger flights as far south as Townsville. Overall, our furthest distance south was to Brisbane. These daily charter flights were to pick up the morning newspapers at around midnight for delivery to all ports north along the eastern seaboard. I spent over 5,000 enjoyable hours flying these routes, first in the old DC-3 referred to as the *covered wagon*, and then in the replacement aircraft, the Fokker F27, nicknamed the *mechanical mouse*.

Taxiing

The tail wheel on the DC-3 is fully castering, with a central locking mechanism, which makes it easier to taxi over long straight distances. Directional control is maintained with both differential power and brakes. However, one technique to avoid is the use of brakes against power. This sometimes happens when the rudder pedals are being used to change direction and one foot slides up, unintentionally, from the rudder bar to the toe brakes.

During taxi, the F/O has the task of holding the control column fully back. This ensures the tail wheel remains firmly in contact with the ground for positive steering and also prevents the aircraft from nosing over if the brakes are applied suddenly. Sometimes, the tail wheel locking device can display some eccentricity and resist removal as a corner is approaching.

The conventional flying controls of the DC-3 play a far more important role when taxiing in windy conditions than they do in modern aircraft. As well as being responsible for ensuring the elevators are held up, the F/O also holds the ailerons into the wind at all times; for example, wind from the left, aileron to the left. Proper use of the flight controls during the taxi also ensures the passengers down the back are not reaching for a sick bag even before becoming airborne. Everything you do up front has an escalating effect toward the tail. As a pilot, once you have traveled in a rear seat, you become a great deal more considerate to those who paid money to sit there.

If used sensibly, differential power is a very powerful tool during the ground handling of the DC-3. While coarse use of rudder is an unavoidable requirement during taxiing, there are times when the pilot runs out of rudder totally, and the only remaining form of control to keep the aircraft straight is an immediate and substantial increase in differential power, perhaps maximum RPM on one engine and idle on the other until control is achieved. When the need for such action becomes apparent, a pretty quick response is necessary, since the end result is an embarrassing ground loop.

When taxiing on water-covered surfaces, the DC-3, on its low-pressure tires, really has a mind of its own, and it is not uncommon to see the runway through the side window as the aircraft skids sideways at right angles to the runway centerline.

Takeoff

After receiving takeoff clearance, with the tail lock in, the throttles are eased forward to their full-power position. Almost immediately, forward pressure is applied to the control column and, as speed is gained, strong corrective rudder is necessary to keep straight due to the gyroscopic effect when the aircraft's tail is raised to its flying position (both engines rotate in the same direction). With the wind down the runway for takeoff, the power is applied evenly; however, if you have a crosswind, it is a good idea to lead with the throttle on the windward (upwind) side, to help counter any weathercock tendency.

Anyone watching a DC-3 break its earthly ties could never describe the accomplishment as a leap skyward, particularly in 95°F heat. That is just the way it is, as all who flew and grew fond of the airplane have discovered.

Airborne

As most would know, the DC-3 has no air conditioning, other than the ability to provide heating for both the cockpit and cabin, and certainly there is no pressurization. So what did we do when flying in the tropics? We would open the cockpit side windows. These days I wonder why we did that, as the incoming air was very hot anyway, not to mention the noise level.

The route structure we were flying called for sixteen takeoffs and landings throughout the day when the temperatures would be more than 95°F. The legs were very short (in one case only five minutes) so the majority of the flying was not above 500 feet. It was not uncommon for the aircraft to be bounced around by the strong summer thermals for three to four hours, while the cabin produced a strong smell of sick bags.

This DC-3 had a *doggie door* set in the main passenger door. Its main purpose is to allow the cabin crew to drop the mail (real airmail) when the airstrips were closed during the wet season. This device did, however, provide an additional service and that was the disposal of used sick bags during these trying summer flights.

(I often wonder what the scriptwriters of that wonderful film *The Gods Must be Crazy*—a story beginning with a bottle that fell from the heavens—could have made of an Australian stockman endeavoring to return a sick bag that fell from the heavens.)

In the monsoon season, plastic raincoats were standard issue, since it could be just as wet inside as it was outside. Yes, the airplane leaked like a sieve, usually in the wrong places, like right over your head or into the middle of your meal or down between your legs, which did little to inspire passenger confidence.

As you can imagine, we were pretty busy throughout the day, with load-sheet calculations and helping with the loading and unloading of the aircraft. All luggage and freight for the front lockers had to be hauled up the inclined passenger aisle since the locker doors were far too high for external loading.

I mentioned the additional noise with the cockpit windows open. This made any cockpit conversation well near impossible and, as checklists still needed to be observed, a silent system was developed by one of our line skippers. It required the F/O to roll the scroll and point to each item, while both the captain and F/O did much head nodding and observing the various actions. To call for the gear down, the PF (pilot flying) gave the thumbs-down sign. Confirming the landing gear lights were green and the gear lever was down and locked was signaled by a thumbs up from both pilots.

Approach and Landing

The most appropriate landing technique for the DC-3 is a tail-down wheeler. The landing gear is substantial, and the wheels are fitted with low-pressure, balloon-type tires. They are about the same size as the main wheels on a DC-9-30, which is configured for 108 passengers while the DC-3 would have room for only 26 passengers. So, with tires this size, the airplane is pretty forgiving during a firm touch down, given there is adequate speed to provide good rudder control during the flare and touchdown.

However, to be slow and to flare too high is a real no-no. Just think about it: you are a couple of feet off the ground with the airspeed reducing, what do you do, keep pulling back or just wait till the airplane drops to the ground?

If you elect to keep applying back pressure, the nose attitude would be higher, further increasing the angle of attack (AOA), finding more lift and perhaps some float (ground effect, reduced induced drag). You are about to enter no-man's-land, losing vision over the nose. (A Concorde nose job would be good.) The tail wheel will probably impact the ground any time now. All the while, as the speed reduces, coarse use of the rudder is necessary to keep her straight. *Bang!* The tail wheel has impacted the ground and pitched the aircraft on to the main wheels and the aircraft sets up a sort of pig root. The airplane heads for the side of the runway. You have full opposite rudder and nothing is happening, although you suspect the bouncing is becoming less.

If you do nothing, there is a good chance of a ground loop. Through out all of this, if the stick is not held back firmly, those pig roots are likely to be exacerbated.

This is all pretty eye-catching when viewed from outside. Waiting passengers observe this most interesting of arrivals and, when they see the faces of the disembarking passengers, they are more than likely to request a refund, rather than risk a flight in this aircraft that bounds about like kangaroo on landing.

Certainly, this is not the most attractive of arrivals; however, a well-executed tail-down wheeler looks great. The approach is a powered one with the power being steadily reduced throughout the flare to touchdown when the throttles are fully closed. The technique is to pick a spot well down the runway and keep that position moving ahead at the same distance throughout the flare and roll out. An initial flare, just as in any other aircraft landing, is essential to reduce the rate of descent to put the aircraft in the landing attitude. Ideally, slight backward pressure is maintained until just prior to when you expect to touch down, then release any backward pressure and the aircraft should roll on perfectly in a slight tail-down attitude.

The pilot then applies forward pressure on the control column, keeping the rudder in the slipstream, until the lack of forward speed prevents the elevators from keeping the tail up in the flying position.

As the tail begins to sink toward the tarmac, there is a need for coarse use of the rudder (loss of slipstream effect) while some differential power or brake might be used to help keep straight. With the DC-3, the old adage that a landing is never over until the aircraft is away in the hangar is especially true, particularly during these final stages of the landing roll.

The most effective crosswind landing technique for the DC-3 is the combination method (crab then wing-down flare). It is a dream machine in a crosswind landing during the approach, flare and initial roll out stages. Most crosswind landings are pretty smooth as the touchdown is made on the upwind wheel. However, in the dying stages of the roll out, when the tail is about to drop down from the flying position, the pilots really need to be on the ball to correct for any weathercocking effect, holding the ailerons into the wind at all times, while the control column is held back firmly to ensure the tail wheel maintains ground contact.

A certainty to spoil any approach and landing is to look down at the runway immediately in front of the aircraft, which results in all manner of mixed landing results. Some pilots use a trickle of power throughout the landing flare, arguing the additional slipstream effect makes just that little bit of difference in the quality of the touchdown.

Afterword

I often remember these flights when younger pilots suggest how marvellous it must have been to fly the DC-3, the Dak. Certainly, anyone who has flown this wonderful airplane received a good grounding in basic aerodynamics every time they went flying. True, the aircraft is slow—we used 120 knots for all flight plans (only two miles a minute), but it worked well enough. However, those who have flown this airplane have sweated a lot, from both physical and mental exertion, particularly in the rainy season with embedded thunderstorms about, no airborne radar, and an ADF not pointing to the NDB until you have passed it. The quality of the operation depends on the individual captain's experience and applied expertise.

I am most grateful to those captains with whom I flew because I learned many tricks of the trade watching how they got the job done legally, safely and in the best interest of their passengers.

Chapter 18

GAF Avro Lincoln (Long-Nose)

By John Laming

General Description

Although none of us will ever get to fly a machine like this four-engine, heavy bomber (except, perhaps, the crew of the B-17 that is still operating), I felt the honest narrative of what it was like to fly such an aircraft would be of interest. I think it is worth recalling such adventures.

The Avro Lincoln was built under license by Australia's Government Aircraft Factory (GAF) after World War II. The Lincoln bomber was the logical development of the Avro Lancaster Bomber used by the British bomber command. The famous raid on the German dams by the 617 Squadron (the *Dambusters*) was carried out by Lancasters.

Australian, New Zealand and British forces were deployed in Malaya during the 1950s to combat communist insurgencies. The Lincoln was active in this campaign and was also assigned the maritime reconnaissance and anti-submarine roles. For these, extra radar operators and observers were needed. The nose section of the Lincoln was modified by the Australian company to provide these crew positions.

The Long-Nose Lincoln was possibly the largest operational taildragger ever built. Sadly, none of these magnificent aircraft remain.

Flight Operations

My first sight of the Avro Lincoln bomber was in April 1953, when I arrived on posting to No. 10 Squadron at Townsville, Northern Australia. The squadron was equipped with 8 Lincolns, a Dakota, Wirraway (T-6), and a Mustang (P-51).

The commanding officer (squadron commander) was Wing Commander John "Handlebars" Handbury AFC, who wore a wide moustache, hence the nickname. Handbury was a charming man, with a gentle manner, who had flown Lockheed Hudsons in New Guinea against the Japanese.

I had experience on Mustangs, Vampires and Wirraways but, as I had not flown any multi-engine aircraft, the Wing Commander explained that I would fly as second pilot on the Lincoln and Dakota for nine months, before being checked out for command.

Six months later, provided I proved competent, I would be given my own crew and operate as a squadron maritime reconnaissance captain. (This was quite unlike the airlines where, at that time, first officers could expect to do 10–15 years in the right-hand seat before offered a command.)

Many of the squadron pilots, navigators, signalers and air gunners had flown over Europe during World War II. Some wore the golden eagle badge of the *Pathfinders* (the guys who went ahead and marked the target for the following waves of bombers; they met the full force of fighters and flak—triple A). Others wore the blue-striped ribbon of the Distinguished Flying Cross. At least two pilots had flown Spitfires.

In fact, I was in august company, although I did not really appreciate the history of those men until many years later when I started to read stories of their wartime exploits in Europe and the Pacific.

The Avro Lincoln began life as the Lancaster Mark 4, but was larger, with a greater bomb load and fuel capacity compared to the early model Lancasters that flew over Europe. Later the name was changed to Lincoln, and many were built under license at Fishermen's Bend in Melbourne, Australia. No. 1 Squadron of the Royal Australian Air Force (RAAF) used these aircraft in bombing raids against the communists in the jungles of Malaya.

My squadron was equipped with the standard bomber, which had four Rolls-Royce Merlin liquid-cooled engines (the same engine fitted to the famous Spitfire). During the early fifties, there was much concern about the advanced capabilities of Russian submarines, and the RAAF decided to modify some Lincolns as submarine hunters. The 2,850 gallons fuel capacity gave over 13 hours' endurance, and the bomb bays were modified to take acoustic-homing torpedoes as well as normal bombs. In order to carry submarine detecting gear, the nose section of these aircraft was lengthened an additional six feet. Additional crew were carried to monitor sonar. This version of the airplane was commonly called the Long-Nose Lincoln. Most of the 3,000 hours I flew in Lincolns were in the Long-Nose.

The aircraft had a maximum weight of 82,000 lbs with conventional gear. It was perhaps the largest operational taildragger ever built. It had all the associated problems of swinging on takeoff and landing. It was particularly difficult to control in crosswinds. Furthermore, because of the long nose, which severely reduced forward vision and reduced directional stability, night landings were fraught with potential for ground loops once the tail was lowered.

Desperate pilots would sometimes be forced to pull down their goggles, yank open the left pilot's sliding window, and shove their faces into the slipstream to locate the left side of the runway flare path. More of this later.

Besides bombs and torpedoes, the Lincoln was initially equipped with a pair of ½-inch caliber machine guns in the nose and rear turrets, plus two 20-millimeter Hispano cannons in the mid-upper turret. A crew of ten was carried for anti-submarine operations.

Both the Lancaster and Lincoln were designed to be flown by one pilot, and I often flew the Lincoln on local flights with only a mechanic or another crew member to help start the engines and keep an eye outside—no specific qualification needed, just another set of hands. (Imagine flying a Jumbo solo.)

The second pilot's seat was a small fold-down seat, known as the *dickey* seat. Anyone wanting to get to the nose compartment was forced to crawl under the dickey seat in the manner of a lizard (flat-out, drinking). The occupant of this seat would have to stand in the aisle for engine start to be able to push all the various buttons needed to start the engines. For takeoff, the seat would be unclipped from the cockpit sidewall, and locked down. There was no shoulder harness for this seat and any severe deceleration would mean that the four large feathering buttons could replace the front teeth of the occupant.

On long flights, we carried a second pilot, as it was obviously no fun to be hand-flying for many hours. The autopilot, affectionately known as George, was a very primitive mechanical device, which required some unusual aircraft maneuvering to get it engaged. Doing this at night, or in cloud, required skill at unusual attitude recoveries.

My first flight was as second pilot in the dickey seat. There had been no type rating, just a hasty reading of the RAF Pilot's Notes. Next flight, I was part of a flypast.

Starting the Merlins

I was to be second pilot on a flight from Townsville to Cairns and return. It was Anzac Day (our special war remembrance day), and we were tasked to fly at 500 feet down the main street of the city, as the parade of servicemen swung past the saluting dais.

The skipper, Sid Gooding, a respected World War II bomber pilot, completed his left-to-right cockpit checks and, after the all-clear, asked me to fire up the starboard inner (no. 3) engine. *Firing-up* was an unfortunate choice of words on that hot and humid 86°F day. I had depressed the primer button for too long and, as the propeller turned over, there was a *whoomph* of igniting 100-octane fuel and long yellow flames licked over the top of the engine from the 12 open exhausts. As the conflagration was only ten feet from my position in the cockpit, it frightened me considerably. However, the calm voice of Sid telling me to stop priming, but keep the propeller turning, calmed me down. Eventually the engine came to life with a roar of Merlin power and the flames were digested. Exhaust fires during start up were a daily fact of life with the Rolls Royce

Merlins, although they were more spectacular than dangerous. Nevertheless, I always felt uneasy when they occurred, particularly at night when the glare of the fire reflected into the cockpit.

With all four engines turning, which pressurized the pneumatic brakes, hydraulically operated flaps and bomb-bay doors, the Captain tested all systems and then taxied for the run-up bay. It was vital to face into the wind for the engine run-up, as the glycol-cooled, in-line Merlins would quickly overheat on the ground. This would cause the coolant to boil, and a spectacular jet of scalding glycol would spurt from the safety valve at the top of the engine. The engine would have to be closed down immediately, otherwise severe damage could result.

Takeoff

That morning, the temperatures remained within limits, and air traffic control cleared us for takeoff. We lined up, straightened the tail wheel, and asked the tail gunner to confirm that his turret was centered, and not traversed to one side. (An offset turret could cause a fair amount of drag to one side, which was not helpful.) All was well and, as the brakes were released with a hiss of compressed air, Sid opened the four throttles to full power with zero boost (30 inches manifold pressure). He paused to ensure that all Merlins responded evenly then, leading with the port outer throttle and with full right rudder to counteract the increasing engine torque effect, Sid increased power on all four to 12 pounds of boost (54 inches manifold pressure).

As speed increased, we gained rudder power and forward pressure on the control wheel gradually raised the tail to a flying attitude. The swing due to the gyroscopic effect of the propellers, which were now showing 3,000 RPM, was easily held by rudder. At 100 knots, Sid eased the Lincoln into the air and called *gear up*. The crackling noise of the four Merlins at full power was physically painful to the ears.

I was pleased when, after the flaps were retracted at 200 feet, I could bring back the throttles and pitch levers to climb boost and revs of 7 pounds and 2,650 RPM, respectively. A check of the top of each engine revealed no sign of coolant blow off (which was reassuring). I had just loosened the throttle friction nut to reduce power, when there was a loud bang from the area of the left wing and the number one throttle jerked sharply under my hand. Sid quietly commented that the port outer engine had failed and that I should feather the propeller without delay. I dithered a little, never having feathered a prop before. But he kept a wary eye on me as I nervously depressed the correct feathering button from a choice of four. (Several years later, I was to be astonished to see all four engines go to feathered from the press of a single feathering button. Fortunately, we were not airborne at the time, but more of that little incident another time.)

The propeller slowly came to a stop and, for the first time in my career, I gazed in wonder at the sight of a feathered propeller. (I was to see many of these during the two tours of duty that I completed on Lincolns.) Meanwhile, Sid must have checked the yaw immediately, because I did not detect any skid, although I was aware of his right hand adjusting the rudder trim. The Lincoln was climbing at 500 fpm as the airspeed settled at 140 knots and we turned left to track comfortably left of the peak on Magnetic Island, which was two miles ahead on runway heading.

(Sid later explained that the no. 1 engine had failed after a blow-back through the induction system. Apparently this was a relatively common occurrence on the Merlin in the tropics, and it always happened without any warning, usually at high power.)

General Handling

The weather forecast was fine and we had allowed some time for some casual coast-crawling (sight-seeing) along the beautiful Queensland coast. The skipper (all Lincoln captains were referred to as *skipper* during flight) had a brief discussion with the navigator regarding time on target at Cairns. Even on three engines, we had time in reserve, so Sid announced that we would press on with the mission. Besides, it was too late to get another Lincoln airborne, and Anzac Day without a visible Air Force presence was unthinkable.

We flew low past the lovely resort islands of Orpheus and Dunk, getting cheery waves from honeymoon couples suntanning on the white sands. A few minutes later, the skipper eased the Lincoln into the channel between the mainland and the jungle-covered slopes of Hinchinbrook Island. Close to the summit of Hinchinbrook, the morning sun reflected off the sad remains of a wartime Liberator that, only a few years before, had flown blindly, at night, into a rock-filled cloud.

The nose gunner reported that he could see crocodiles ahead lazing in the mangrove swamps. A few seconds later the rear gunner told us that he could see splashes in the shallows as these prehistoric monsters, alarmed by the sight and sound of a pterodactyl with four Merlins, scrambled for deeper water.

Flyby

Approaching Cairns, we received clearance from ATC for a low run over the airport. A minute later our Lincoln, with its port outer propeller feathered, flew down the main street of Cairns right on time as the marching veterans of two world wars made a smart eyes-right toward the saluting dais. Our task completed, the navigator gave the skipper a course for home. Sid was getting a bit tired by now, as the Lincoln on three engines was quite a handful, especially as the foot load on the rudders was high. I was given control in the right-hand seat, while the skipper relaxed with a flask of hot tea and some sandwiches.

The aircraft was quite heavy on the controls and I had some difficulty holding an accurate heading with asymmetric power. This was exacerbated by having to look across the width of the vast cockpit to read the compass, which was situated directly in front of the captain. The Lincoln was designed to be operated by one pilot, with the occasional assistance of an engineer who would sit on the dickey seat at a lower level than the pilot. All flight instruments were directly in front of the pilot, of course. It was never designed to be flown from the right seat. All I had in front of me were four feathering buttons with their associated fire warning lights, a swag of starter, priming and booster coil buttons, various armament selectors, a supercharger control switch, and a mixture control assembly with four switches. None of it was useful in flying the airplane.

Sid encouraged me to try a few steep turns, which brought a chorus of protests over the intercom. The navigator was complaining because I was ruining his neat plotting chart by causing him to spill his coffee. The rear gunner, who had vacated his turret, was angry because he was crouching over the Elsen (toilet pan), and my flying was affecting his aim. The rest of the crew were annoyed because they were either trying to have lunch, or have a siesta.

Sid resumed control for the last leg into Townsville. We deviated a mile or so to fly at 100 feet along the beaches of the aboriginal settlement of Palm Island. The locals waved merrily, and Sid returned the compliment with wing-waggling and a steep wingover. The navigator gave the skipper the final course for Townsville.

The early Lincolns were not equipped with a radio compass, and instrument let-downs were done by a talk-down, using ground control approach (GCA) radar, or ATC-operated VHF radio direction-finding. As the aircraft was equipped with only one VHF radio, the situation could become serious if the radio failed in bad weather. En route navigation was carried out by the specialist navigator using sextant sightings of the sun or stars with sometimes Loran, HF/DF and basic dead-reckoning (DR) plotting. At some RAAF fields, we could home to the station using a primitive wartime pulse-radar beacon called *Lucero*. Like most newly graduated pilots of that era, I had complete faith in the ability of all navigators. Yet, as I grew more experienced, I realized that they could be just as uncertain of the true position of the aircraft, and equally apprehensive of bad weather, as I was.

(Two years later, the crew and passengers of one of our Long-Nose Lincolns were killed when the aircraft crashed into Mount Superbus at night while letting down in cloud. The bomber was over sixty miles off track while heading for Brisbane on a medical evacuation flight from Townsville. The let-down was done on DR as the aircraft had been flying in cloud for several hours, which made astronavigation impossible. After that accident, I realized that navigators were not Supermen, and I began to take an active interest in knowing roughly the position of my aircraft at all times, especially at night or in cloud.)

Approach and Landing

Meanwhile, in the pattern, we joined downwind for an asymmetric landing for runway 02. A hill called Mount Louisa was inconveniently situated one mile from the threshold and on mid-base leg. It was 700 feet high. With a nice touch, Sid brought the Lincoln in a curve inside the hill, straightening up at 500 feet for the final approach.

Crossing the fence at 105 knots, Sid closed the throttles, the Merlins gave their characteristic *snap, crackle* and *pop*, and the aircraft greased on. There was a gentle hissing of pneumatic brakes as Sid squeezed the brake lever, and I watched the brake pressure needle drop a few psi from 450 lbs. Anything less than 150 psi total accumulator pressure was considered not a good thing, especially as the charging rate of the engine-driven pneumatic system was notoriously slow at taxi engine RPM.

From the height of my seat above ground level, I spotted what appeared to be the burned out wreckage of an aircraft near the western boundary of the airport. The only recognizable part was the twin fin and rudders, which identified it as a Lincoln. Initially, I thought it must have been a wreck used by the firecrew for practice.

After engine shutdown, we unloaded our parachutes, Mae Wests (life vests), and navigation bags and clambered down the ladder from the front escape hatch. The gunners and radio operators had an easier exit via the rear entry door. The humidity made us sweat profusely but, as there were no crew showers in those days, we simply stepped out of our sodden green flying suits into our khaki drab uniforms smelling like polecats.

Afterword

Before we went for debriefing, I asked Sid about the wreckage I had seen on the airfield boundary. He said that it was all his own work, having pranged the aircraft during an asymmetric overshoot two weeks earlier. Considering his war experience, and my personal observations of his undoubted skills as a Lincoln pilot, I was most surprised at this revelation. I asked him what had happened.

It appears he was demonstrating an asymmetric landing with the port outer propeller feathered. The crew consisted of Sid as the qualified flying instructor (QFI), another pilot who was undergoing conversion to type, and a signaler. There was a 10-knot crosswind from the right, and during the flare the aircraft began to drift left off the runway. The Lincoln was difficult to land in crosswinds, as are most tail wheel types. The long nose of the Lincoln Mk 31 also obscured the view of the runway from the cockpit.

Sid was unable to stop the Lincoln from drifting off the runway edge and decided to go around rather than risk landing gear damage from sideways drift. He applied full power on the three remaining engines. This caused a strong yaw towards the feathered number one propeller. It was a classic V_{MCA} situation, and with full-right rudder applied Sid was unable to stop the aircraft from turning left. At that stage the Lincoln was flying ten feet above the airfield in ground effect, but in a huge circle. Thirty seconds later the left wing tip clipped a small power pole near the airfield perimeter. The aircraft spun around and crashed with the remaining engines at full throttle. Apart from the signaler who broke his nose against the radio panel, there were no injuries and the crew fled from the scene. A minute later, the Lincoln caught fire and, despite the efforts of the fire crew, the aircraft was totally destroyed.

Chapter 19

Hawker Sea Fury

By John Laming

General Description

The Hawker Sea Fury can rightly be called the ultimate piston-engine fighter aircraft. It evolved from the Fury (the ultimate biplane fighter), the famous Hurricane, Typhoon and Tempest—a potent series of fighter planes.

The Sea Fury was the naval fighter version of the Tempest and entered service at the end of the World War II. It served in Korea with the Australian and British navies. One is credited with a MiG kill.

Some were modified for unlimited pylon racing in the U.S. Several survive as warbirds.

Flight Operations

After graduation as a sergeant pilot, in December 1952, I was posted to the Australian fighter base at Williamtown, north of Sydney, to fly Mustangs (P-51) and de Havilland Vampires. While I enjoyed the hack, rack, flick and zoom thing, I was a lousy shot and sadly lacked the skills needed to be a true fighter pilot. I could bracket a tank with my rockets, but never hit it! Despite spraying bullets all over the firing range, I rarely hit the target. I blamed poor harmonization of the machine guns, which I suspected were set to 250 miles instead of 250 yards.

My squadron commander, a thoughtful ex-Spitfire pilot, wisely decided that Australia would be safer with me as a bomber pilot, where I was unlikely to hurt anyone with stray bullets. And so I was posted to fly Lincolns at Townsville. To my delight there was a Mustang on strength, but its guns had been removed and I was unable to practice my firing skills. Swamp crocodiles could rest in peace and the bombing range on Rattlesnake Island would remain a safe haven for wildlife. The Mustang was modified for target-towing and, besides flying Lincolns, I spent many hours towing a drogue at which air gunners fired cannon shells. With relief, tempered by moments of fear, I realized I was not the only lousy shot in the Air Force.

Our primary task was to chase foreign submarines. The tame ones were based at Sydney and we would fly to the RAN base at Nowra to practice the art of submarine hunting. Each year we were allowed to drop one Mk 34 homing torpedo aimed at an acoustic buoy that made submarine noises. Torpedoes were expensive, the defence budget tight, and so we saw the annual torpedo drop (all of five minutes) as a momentous occasion.

The torpedo, launched from the Lincoln at 200 feet, would hit the sea, then go feral, circling the unfortunate buoy before arrowing in with the ferocity of a white pointer. On hitting the buoy, it would broach the surface, then continue to circle until lining up for another go. After five minutes, it would run out of puff and float lazily on the surface until retrieved by a waiting rescue launch. Overhead, the Lincoln would steep turn to allow the crew to see the results of a year in waiting for this precious moment. Intelligence reports later revealed that most Russian submarines could out-run our torpedoes, hence the exercise was somewhat academic.

In October 1953, I flew to the Nowra Naval Air Station to undergo training in anti-submarine warfare. I wandered down to the hangars to look at the airplanes. I saw lines of Sea Furies and Fireflies. In the hangars, were Venoms and Wirraways plus a Dakota, an Auster, and some Wessex helicopters.

A few months earlier in Darwin, I had neatly stood a Wirraway (Aussie T-6), on its nose, when the brakes jammed. Notwithstanding, I decided to ask permission to borrow a Navy Wirraway for some general flying practice. You could do that sort of thing in those days; in fact, it was encouraged, to give young military pilots wider experience. Nowadays, it is "no way, no money."

The flight commander was a delightful chap. He was very enthusiastic about the idea and said, "Oh! So you have flown Mustangs, eh? Well, forget the Wirraway. How about a Fury instead?"

I could hardly believe my ears and quickly accepted his offer, little realizing what I had let myself in for. He handed me the pilot's notes: "Read this Sergeant and, after lunch, we'll fix you up."

Preflight

I spent the next two hours avidly cramming. Page 40, paragraph 63 gave advice on spinning:

Intentional spinning is prohibited. Should an accidental spin occur, normal recovery action should be applied immediately and a speed of 175 knots should be attained before recovery from the resulting dive is attempted.

Must remember that one, I thought, in case I get a bit careless with aerobatics, for which paragraph 65 tabled the various speeds. Loops were flown at 320–360 knots, and upward rolls at 350–400 knots. Heady speeds indeed after the 165-knot cruise speed of the stately Lincoln, although you could get 300 knots in a dive while pretending not to notice the flexing of the wings.

Like most British engines, power was indicated as pounds of boost per square inch, rather than in manifold pressure in inches of mercury as with American aircraft. Zero boost equaled 30 inches of mercury.

Having enjoyed the condemned pilot's last meal in the petty officers' mess, I straightened my tie and marched down the hill to the tarmac at 1300 hours. My allotted aircraft, Sea Fury RAN 920 with its wings smartly folded in salute, was among several others on line. A sub-lieutenant of my own age briefed me on emergencies, general flying, takeoff technique and go-around procedure. Time dims the finer details of that briefing, but I still remember a few vital points.

"First thing to remember on takeoff is that it swings right," said the sub-lieutenant.

"For that reason, avoid opening the throttle too fast and don't push the tail up too early. Use +9 boost and rich mixture cuts in at +4. That's when the swing will occur. Take off with the canopy in the open position in case of engine failure after takeoff. And very important: when you wind the canopy shut don't let your hand slip off the handle, because if it does, the airflow will slam the canopy forward and hit the back of your head. We lost a pilot last year because of that. Finally, no spins please, and 90 knots over the fence."

Sounded like good advice, except that I felt that 90 knots over the fence was a bit slow for such a big fighter, especially after the 105 knots I had used in Mustangs. Still, I assumed that the sub-lieutenant knew what he was talking about and asked no more questions. Throwing my parachute nonchalantly over one shoulder I accompanied my mentor to the flight line. Approaching the aircraft, I got that nervous flutter in the pit of my stomach and wondered, "Did I really want to fly this brute with its 2,500-hp Centaurus engine and massive five-blade propeller?"

Close up, I was surprised how high from the ground was the cockpit and how small in comparison with the size of the aircraft. I needed more time to familiarize myself with the cockpit layout and, too late, began to think that perhaps I should have stuck with the Wirraway.

The walk-around complete, I climbed into the cockpit assisted by the sub-lieutenant and a naval rating known as a *pilot's mate*. After a further discussion on start procedures, I was ready to go.

Starting

The staring sequence for the Sea Fury is initiated by carrying out a left-to-right check (in Boeings, this is called the *scan*). Confirm that the ignition switch is off, main fuel cock on, throttle one-inch open, supercharger control in low gear, and parking brake on. Next prime the cylinders, turn the ignition on, select the cartridge starter, and get the all-clear to start. That done, press the combined starter and booster coil push-button.

On that day at Nowra, this resulted in a muffled explosion, a cloud of black smoke and a few revolutions of the propeller. Then the engine simply stopped. The sub-lieutenant, who was standing on the port wing leaning into the cockpit, muttered something about a jammed starter solenoid. He called this news down to the pilot's mate, who had been standing, at ease, by the starboard wing with his hands behind his back. The mate leaped, Tarzan-like, onto the starboard wheel and, from there, onto the wing. Astonished, I saw him produce a rubber mallet and give a resounding whack to the engine cowl in front of the windscreen. This presumably freed the offending solenoid and, after springing back to the ground, the mate gave me the thumbs up for another start.

After a second cartridge was placed in the firing chamber, I checked all-clear and pressed the starter button. There was another big bang with accompanying smoke and the propeller made more desultory turns and stopped. Soot from the cartridge exhaust drifted over the white uniform of the sub-lieutenant who was still standing on the wing, and scowling at this latest turn of events. As it turned out, I had forgotten to turn on the separate ignition switch. *Guilty as charged, Your Honor!*

A third cartridge was selected, ignition switched on, throttle set, and I pressed the starter button. A big bang as the cartridge fired and *magnifique!*, the propeller spun and the engine caught on all 18 cylinders. Adjusting the throttle to idle, I turned to the sub-lieutenant only to see him hopping around on the ground having been blown off the wing by the slipstream! I nearly wept with laughter. Selecting the wing-folding lever, I watched, fascinated, as the wings slowly lowered into place.

On my signal, the pilot's mate withdrew the wheel chocks and gave me a salute from the safety of the starboard wing tip. The sub-lieutenant had already exited stage left, shaking his head in disbelief.

Taxiing

Having received taxi instructions from the tower controller, I released the tail wheel lock and swung out of the parking line. The long nose of the Sea Fury meant that I had to continuously weave to check ahead, meanwhile keeping an eye on the brake air pressure gauge. Each squeeze of the brake lever depleted the air reservoir and, at idle RPM, the air compressor was inefficient. You could lose braking. Exhaust smoke was being drawn into the cockpit by the slipstream, and it was necessary to wear the oxygen mask while taxiing.

After being cleared for takeoff, I did a final check of the trims, ensured the canopy was locked open, adjusted the seat, noted the position of the airspeed indicator and muttered a small incantation to the patron saint of pilots.

Takeoff

As I cautiously opened the throttle, I noticed two red fire tenders on either side of the runway, their occupants dressed in asbestos suits (or whatever they wore in those days), helmets on and ready for battle. These chaps were serious about their job and, as I began the takeoff roll, both tenders initially kept up till about 40 knots, and then rapidly fell behind. With full left rudder trim, it was easy to keep straight with coarse rudder, while the acceleration was similar to that experienced in a Mustang. I had just raised the tail, when I momentarily lost sight of the airspeed indicator. Engrossed in keeping straight and with the shattering noise of 2,500 hp belting my ears, I was beyond the normal 100-knot takeoff speed when I found the airspeed indicator again.

After lifting off, I realized that the beast was airborne at less than half throttle. If you think that improbable, then page three of the pilot's notes states: "Full throttle should always be used for takeoff, even though the aircraft may become airborne before a full throttle position is reached."

Airborne

Now off the deck, I hurriedly pushed the throttle to full takeoff power. As it went through the rich mixture cut-in point of +4 boost, the extra torque caused a rapid roll. I picked the wing up smartly and tried to raise the gear. This was no mean feat, as being rather short and, with a locked shoulder harness, I could barely reach the lever. The lever could only be raised after a safety catch was unlatched and this was a tricky one-finger effort. The Fury porpoised a few times as I groped for the safety catch and gear lever combination with my right hand, while I transferred my left hand from the throttle to the stick. (This ridiculous switching of hands at a critical moment of takeoff was a feature of several British fighters, including the Spitfire.) Finally, I got the gear up and pulled the propeller pitch control back into what would normally be full coarse pitch on most aircraft, but which was called *auto* in the Sea Fury. Henceforth, the propeller pitch was controlled automatically by the throttle. Climbing at 165 knots and passing 1,500 feet, I swapped hands to close the canopy.

What happened then, beggars belief. I was wearing a standard-issue cloth helmet to which my goggles were attached by an elastic band. While winding the canopy handle forward my gloved hand slipped and the handle ran free under aerodynamic load. I ducked instinctively, remembering in a flash the warning from the sub-lieutenant of the lethality of an unlocked free-sliding canopy. The canopy slammed shut missing my head, but catching the top of my goggles. I was jerked up by the elastic band and by the force of the slipstream tugging against the goggles, which were whipping around outside the canopy. I lost sight of the instrument panel, seeing nothing but blue sky while by now the Fury was accelerating and getting badly out of trim. I was up the proverbial creek, not game to let go of the stick (in order to use both hands to force the canopy open). I was now losing my sense of humor. It was replaced by fear.

In between straining with my neck to break clear of the goggles, and groping for the elevator trim to relieve the stick pressures, my head was twanged back hard several times against the top of the canopy. Meanwhile, the Sea Fury was rocketing skyward at 3,000 feet per minute.

Fortunately, after one more savage neck pull, the elastic band snapped and my goggles disappeared below, leaving me with a sore neck and high pulse rate.

Having regained my lost dignity, I now enjoyed myself doing steep turns, stalls in the landing configuration (I was a bit worried about spinning, in case I screwed-up the recovery), and a few aerobatic maneuvers.

Apart from the high cockpit noise level, the Sea Fury proved a beautiful aircraft to fly. I was surprised at how short the wings looked from the cockpit and the feather lightness of the controls even at 400 knots. The rate of roll was impressive and, in retrospect, I preferred the Sea Fury to the Mustang. I felt, however, that the Mustang would be more forgiving in a wheels-up landing. Trying different power settings I found that, at maximum-range configuration, the aircraft steadied at 195 knots with only 1,400 RPM. With climb power for aerobatics, the speed quickly reached 400 knots, with an acceleration in a dive near that of a Vampire. I was tempted to do a vertical climbing roll, but again the thought of an inadvertent spin made me cautious, so I satisfied myself instead with numerous barrel rolls.

Just before one slow roll, I aimed the Fury at a cloud for nose reference and was startled to see another aircraft coming at me head on. I broke violently then straightened up long enough to look over the port wing. Nothing seen in that direction. Glancing ahead through the bullet-proof windscreen, I again saw the same aircraft. Relieved and feeling slightly foolish, I realized that it was only a squashed insect on the windscreen.

Approach and Landing

It was time to go home. I had trouble opening the canopy, but finally got it locked while turning onto the final approach. The long nose began to block my view of the runway as I caught a glimpse of the fire tenders beginning to move. Then came the second unforgettable moment of my flight. Passing the threshold, I closed the throttle and flared.

To this day, I swear it looked nice to me, my speed was right on 90 knots, it was a calm day, and I really thought I could not miss. But, to my horror, the Sea Fury ran out of elevator, bounced heavily onto the main wheels and back into the air, and seemed to leave me with no choice but to go around. Visions of a full-power torque roll made me change my mind and I was fortunate to recover with a burst of power and frantic juggling of the stick. After that, all went well, although the aircraft seemed to slow up quickly once the tail was down.

Meanwhile, the fire tenders on the grass verge had shot past me and must have misjudged my stopping speed, judging from the clods of earth torn up by their skidding wheels as they changed down through a thousand gears.

The penny dropped when I realized that, after the first bounce, I had inadvertently squeezed the brake lever on the control column, landing with the brakes partially on. No wonder the aircraft pulled up faster than anticipated by the fire tenders.

In Retrospect

A few years later, I was back at Nowra. I was now a flight lieutenant, which is one stripe more than a sub-lieutenant. There was a Sea Fury on the tarmac and we were not leaving till later that evening. So I walked down the hill to the tarmac and said hello to the senior pilot.

"Oh, so you have flown the Fury before?" asked the senior pilot, a navy commander. "Did you enjoy it, old man?"

"Yes, I loved it," I said (trying to sound nonchalant). "Any chance of a short flight?" I added.

"No problem," said the man.

This time I was offered Sea Fury RAN 893, issued with a helmet and briefed by the duty sub-lieutenant to use "around 105 knots over the fence, seeing it's your first trip in a Fury for a few years."

This threshold speed suited me fine. I told him that my previous mentor said to use 90 knots. The sub-lieutenant was shocked and said that it was fortunate that I did not bend the aircraft, because 90 knots was just above the stall and used strictly for carrier landings.

Back then, I must have missed page 42, paragraph 6b(d) of the Sea Fury Pilot's Notes, which reads, "The recommended speed for deck landing is 90–92 knots. It is necessary to pull the control column well back to effect a three-point touchdown."

I am still looking for that first sub-lieutenant.

This flight in the Sea Fury was without drama and I enjoyed every minute, greasing the Fury with a tail-high wheeler landing. I have flown many different types of aircraft since those days and, at the time I first drafted this article, I was happily driving the delightful Boeing 737 around the South Pacific skies.

Now, long since retired to the safe job as a flight simulator instructor, I would give the world to be able to renew my acquaintance with a Sea Fury—minus the earlier frights, of course. Oh, to be young again.

Chapter 20

Piper Pawnee

By John Freeman

General Description

The original Piper Pawnee was an agricultural airplane developed from the Super Cub. It was basically the Cub with the wing on the bottom, the strut on the top, the pilot in the rear cockpit and the spray tank filling the forward cockpit. It grew from there in terms of power and payload.

The Pawnee PA–25–235 became the major agricultural model. Many retired Pawnees world-wide are also used to aerotow sailplanes. They are a popular airplane.

Piper Pawnee PA-25-235

The 235 moved through four models, A, B, C and D, with minor changes until the D model. This model saw the fuel tank, which in the earlier models was very hazardously located immediately behind the engine, separated into two wing tanks, each just outboard of the strut attachment on each wing. The 235 is powered by a Lycoming O-540 engine of 235 hp, with a fixed-pitch Macauley metal propeller. Some models are available with 260 hp and a constant-speed propeller, but the 235-hp engine, being a de-rated O-540, and the simplicity of the fixed-pitch propeller makes an ideal combination for any agricultural job ranging from one acre to 1,000 acres.

The Pawnee has an all-metal structure with some metal skins, but in the main was fabric covered. Its hopper holds up to 140 gallons (650 liters) which, when full, and with full fuel tanks, takes the aircraft over its design maximum weight.

Flight Operations

When operating from a bumpy airstrip with a full load, the contents tend to leak out of the hopper top-filling door and onto the windscreen. Just like World War I!

The landing gear is strong, the shock being absorbed by bungee cords, but some aircraft have air-filled shock struts. The cockpit position is great. The long nose is level with the ground in the tail-down attitude, which gives an excellent view from its high-set single cockpit while on the ground, and an even better view ahead when in the flying attitude. In fact, at 6–8 feet spraying height, one can see the ground some 100 yards ahead when looking straight over the nose. Fabulous. Its large main wheels and sprung tail wheel make for a comfortable ride even on rough fields. Disk brakes and sprung tail wheel steering make for easy maneuvering on the ground. In the air the control response is excellent in all three axes, the rudder and elevator being very positive. However, it is possible to run out of aileron authority in gusty conditions.

The cockpit offers toe brakes, widely spaced rudder pedals, well-placed control column and fast-acting elevator trim (from full nose-down to full tail-down by winding a trim handle on the left-hand side for only two turns). The trim operates via spring tension applied to the elevator cables. The pilot is restrained by a four-point shoulder harness with inertia reel—lockable or free. Simple throttle, mixture and carburetor heat controls are clustered on a left-hand throttle quadrant.

There is a basic panel comprising engine primer, magneto switches, airspeed indicator, altimeter, turn and balance indicator, cylinder-head temperature gauge, combined oil temperature and pressure gauges, ammeter, circuit breakers, landing/taxi light switch, instrument panel light switch, starter button and master switch. The pilot is protected by a roll bar (turn-over truss). Cockpit heating is available; cooling is by a simple vent above the pilot's head.

Starting

Starting is carried out by priming the engine, with mixture set to rich, with four strokes of the engine primer (or, more often, six strokes of the throttle). Then the sequence is stick back, brakes on, left (impulse) magneto switch on, master switch on, and starter engaged. The hot start is with two primes of the throttle.

Warm up at 1,000 RPM. If carburetor icing is possible, it is most important to select carburetor heat. The Pawnee is very susceptible to carburetor icing. At idle RPM, with the carburetor heat set to cold, the carburetor can slowly ice up and the engine stop. This susceptibility also applies when airborne and, in cool or humid conditions, it is wise to apply carburetor heat every 20 minutes or so.

Taxiing

Taxiing either into wind, crosswind or downwind is simple in the Pawnee as its large wheels, disk brakes and steerable tail wheel have great authority. The low wing does not lift too much.

Takeoff

Takeoff is made with or without flap. The simple flaps are behind the main wheels and positioned where stone damage may occur. However, when fully laden, the first stage of 10° flap means lifting off the ground 100 yards earlier. It is a call you must make at the time. Crosswind takeoff is simple as, with the long nose, an equal area of keel surface exists in front and behind the center of gravity. Into-wind aileron is applied as usual and, in strong crosswind conditions, the Pawnee tends to "walk" slightly sideways to the downwind side of the strip, but it does not swing.

General Handling

In the air, the aircraft is easily turned, medium or steep, and has an excellent field of view. The wings-level stall is simple, with or without flap, with a positive nose-drop to the glide attitude. Even when spraying equipment is fitted, there is no tendency for one wing to drop before the other. Approaching a stall in the turn should be exercised with caution. Recovery must always be by relaxing back pressure on the control column to unstall the wing followed by rudder only to stop any roll or yaw. Any attempt to use aileron to roll level in this situation may cause the lower wing to stall and the upper wing to keep lifting, with the result that the aircraft rolls to level, but inverted!

Approach and Landing

Approach and landing in the Pawnee is simple. The view over the nose is excellent as the aircraft approaches at 70 knots using full flap (40°). The aircraft is easily flared to a level nose attitude and then touches down in a three-point attitude. It then rolls quite straight with the tail wheel steering and excellent braking completing the task.

Crosswinds

In crosswind conditions, the crab technique works well: lay off drift and yaw the aircraft straight just before touchdown. Into-wind aileron may also be used after touchdown, particularly in strong crosswinds. The maximum crosswind component for the Pawnee is 15 knots. It is wise for the new pilot to be familiar with the level flight attitude on the ground by taxiing for 5 or 10 minutes prior to takeoff to recognize and remember the correct attitude for landing. Any attempt to raise the nose further in the flare will result in the tail wheel touching down first.

Summary

The Pawnee is a simple aircraft to operate, a joy to fly, has excellent visibility and good ground handling characteristics. It is built to work, but there is no law against enjoying work—is there?

Anecdotes

An Easy Life

I was returning to base one afternoon from an operational site some 80 miles distant, cruising at 1,000 feet in calm conditions. I flew along with my feet on the flat cockpit floor of the Pawnee as it flew so straight that rudder was not needed. On arrival, I joined the pattern, turned onto the base leg, then onto final approach, selected flap and continued my approach to flare height. I arrived gently on three points. I rolled down the strip and, when I decided to brake, I found that my feet were still flat on the floor. It was no problem. There was plenty of time to move them to the rudder and brake pedals. It shows how simple and straightforward the approach and landing is in the Pawnee, with the tail wheel steering springs almost acting like a tail wheel lock to keep the aircraft straight.

Time Slows Down

One morning, when ferrying a short distance from the overnight airstrip to an operational airstrip in the Adelaide Hills, I smelled oil/smoke. The Pawnee has an oil filter with a cork gasket beneath the lid that is held by a bolt vertically through the lid to the base. At times, the gasket becomes worn resulting in the lid chattering and the gasket breaking up. This allows oil to escape and to leak onto the engine exhaust muffler causing smoke.

Very little oil is usually lost and a prompt return to the airstrip to replace the gasket solves the problem. This morning, however, I looked at the oil pressure gauge and was very alarmed to see it was dropping. The gasket had failed on engine warm up and leaked much oil. With takeoff power, the leaking oil warmed to the extent of producing smoke, leaving little oil in the engine. It was quite early in the day and the sky to the east (just before sunrise) was very bright so I could not turn that way. It was too dark to see any fields for landing.

The only other option was to turn to the west and to look down-sun. With dropping oil pressure, I had to land immediately. I could not get back to the departure airstrip. I could just make out two trees at the end of a small field I had sprayed the previous year when it was in potatoes, and I knew that it was not grass (local knowledge is wonderful!).

At this point everything slowed down. With the throttle closed and 600 RPM, I could see the propeller blades as they turned, I... glanced... at... the... oil... pressure... gauge... and... saw... 15 psi... and... knew... the... engine... would... be... alright,... turned on... the... landing... light,... sideslipped... over... some... wires... on... the... road... at... the... edge... of... the... field... forward... slipped... away... my... airspeed... and... arrived... on... the... ground,... braked... harshly,... ground... looped... with... my... wing... on... the... end... fence... wire.

At this point everything sped up again. I shut down, climbed out and my legs collapsed. I had landed successfully in a four-acre field in almost dark conditions without damaging the aircraft. The wonderful Pawnee saved my day.

Chapter 21

Pitts Special

By David Pilkington

General Description

The original Pitts Special was a small, single-seat, homebuilt biplane of the 1940s. It was designed by Curtis Pitts and was originally powered by a 55-hp engine. The airplane was found to be responsive and very, very strong. It became a standard aerobatic mount for budding champions and won many contests. The engine was progressively upgraded to 150 hp and then to 260 hp! A two-seat version was also built. The Pitts was manufactured commercially as well as being built from plans.

The most common Pitts in Australia are the single-seat S-1S and the two-seat S-2A. Few of the later model, the S-2B, have reached this country.

The current production Pitts is the S-2C. It is the one that I know particularly well as I was a major contributor to the design as vice-president of engineering at Aviat Aircraft throughout the initial design and prototype construction phase. Until the S-2C appeared in 1998, the S-2B had been in production since the early 1980s with very little in the way of design changes until we introduced the 50th Anniversary Limited Edition S-2B-50 in 1996.

The S-2B-50 featured the same six-cylinder, 260-hp Lycoming engine, same flying surfaces and same fuselage, but introduced the new landing gear, tighter cowl, three-blade composite propeller and improved cockpit features, such as eyeball fresh-air vents, electronic instrumentation, electronic fuel gauge, improved panel layout and secondary controls. The prototype S-2B-50 in fact became the prototype S-2C with new flying surfaces: beefed up wings with long span ailerons, squared-off wing tips and squared-off tail surfaces.

Flight Operations

The two-seat Pitts features a tandem cockpit with the command pilot seated in the rear. At first, it seems that all that can be seen is the back of your passenger's head and a long engine cowl. Second and third impressions are much the same: this is definitely one airplane where you need to S-turn while taxiing.

Except for early-model S-2As, where only one cockpit was enclosed, a full-length jettisonable canopy covers both cockpits.

When wearing a parachute be particularly careful that you do not damage the canopy as you slink in. Once you are in, ensure that the canopy is properly closed and latched, otherwise it will depart of its own accord at a time convenient to itself.

Starting

Upon start-up, the rumble of the Lycoming and the propeller slipstream tickling the flying surfaces emphasizes that this has a high power-to-weight ratio: it wants to fly and spend as little time on the ground as possible.

Looking out to the wing tip, it seems so close that you could almost reach your hand out and touch it. It just does not seem like enough wing, so forget that and concentrate on the front: there is plenty of airframe there to see and you will usually be going the same direction as the nose is pointed. So, look ahead.

It is worthwhile taking the time to taxi around for a long time before flying a Pitts for the first time. Become familiar with the cockpit and controls, the external visual cues and the three-point ground attitude. This will stand you in good stead for your landings.

Takeoff

If you have had some good tail wheel instruction in other types, you will not find the takeoff in a Pitts to be a problem, but you will find it exciting. Even the 200-hp, two-seat Pitts will give you a kick in the pants, having you accelerating quickly down the runway and off the ground before you really have a chance to appreciate it.

Best rate-of-climb speed for the S–2C is 82 knots but, especially if you are at a busy airport, a cruise climb of 105 knots will give you much better view of other traffic. The objective of your first flight should be general familiarization with the handling characteristics, which will without doubt impress you. It really is docile and well behaved in the air. It also goes right where you point it. The rate of climb is something like 2,200 feet per minute—you will not find a VSI on the panel, though.

Maximum level speed is quoted as 165 knots but, at that speed, you will be burning 31.7 gallons per hour out of a tank that holds 33 gallons usable. A more practical cruise at 65% power burns only 18–21 gallons per hour at 145 knots. With the 7-gallon wing tank, you have a safe range of about 200 NM. Pilots do not normally take out a Pitts to go touring, though. As Aviat's publicity blurb says:

> … it has been the omnipresent American aerobatic machine for generations. In fact, it seems impossible that it has been over half a century since the first of the little pug-nosed acrobugs took to the air with 55 wheezing horses up front.

Aerobatics

Looking at the aerobatic placard in the cockpit is a good clue to how much fun you can have in this airplane. The list of outside maneuvers is identical to the inside maneuvers. This airplane does not care which way up it is. Each maneuver has a wide range of recommended entry speeds. Loop anywhere from 113 to 156 knots. Slow roll anywhere between 87 and 156 knots. Snap roll anywhere between 78 and 122 knots. It goes around rolls as if it was on rails. You will be kicking your old aerobatic instructor for not telling you how easy they could be in a Pitts.

I used to enjoy demonstrating the S–2B to first-time Pitts pilots. I will never forget one experienced Decathlon aerobatic instructor who started off a slow roll using about a one-third aileron deflection. He then told me that he would use full aileron on the next one. That would whip us around at about 240 degrees per second. That is fast enough to give you some serious bruising from hitting the side of the cockpit in a hesitation roll! However, I was not quite prepared for what happened next: he applied a lot of forward stick as well as a lot of aileron; so much forward stick that we both lost our headsets as he pushed −5G in what became a violent outside barrel roll.

That flexibility in entry speed and ease of accomplishing basic aerobatics just makes it so tempting to put together a sequence for a contest or display. Of course, every Pitts display must include the maneuver at which the Pitts excels: the lomcevàk. It is not difficult and, as one of my friends used to say, "all you need is a heavy hand and a Pitts."

Spinning

When I redesigned the cockpit layout, one of the things I just had to move was the no-smoking placard as it was using prime real estate: front and center of the main panel. Although there was a regulation requiring such a placard, it did not seem to me as if there would be a risk if that placard was less prominent. My thought was that the spinning and aerobatic placards were most important. Spinning is one flight regime where many pilots have come to grief in the Pitts. There is absolutely no question that the Pitts will recover readily from any spin that it is possible to get it into, whether steep, flat, accelerated, upright or inverted.

For many pilots, the first session of serious spinning is likely to result in spatial disorientation. Do not make your first such experience solo. Optimum recovery action from the flat spins is significantly different than the standard spin recovery you would have been taught with your basic spin training. In fact, the standard spin recovery technique would just have you spinning forever. Falling out of even a basic aerobatic maneuver can easily result in an inadvertent inverted flat spin, so advanced spinning tuition is an essential part of a Pitts checkout.

Approach and Landing

The current production model, the S-2C is the easiest of all the Pitts to land. Regardless of that, all the Pitts rate high in terms of excitement on landing. The short wing span and high power-to-weight ratio results in a high performance with lively control response. The poor forward visibility, absence of flaps, narrow landing gear, stiff bungee gear and short tail arm makes for landing characteristics as per the book for tail wheel airplanes. Yes, the Pitts exhibits classical behavioral characteristics, but be warned, it is at the extreme end of the book.

Personally, I have not taken much interest in wheel landings in the Pitts, so I will admit up front there are better Pitts pilots than myself. (But, while I'm here, I will pass on a tip with wheel landings in the Pitts: put one main wheel on the ground first to significantly reduce the tendency to bounce.)

Therefore, with the Pitts, I prefer to see the classic three-point touchdown, but let's back up to the start of the approach. In the U.S., Pitts pilots prefer the carrier-style approach pattern: 800 feet altitude on downwind, close enough that the wing tip is "on" the runway and, when abeam the piano keys, a curved base/final leg is commenced. In the model S-2B, an airspeed of around 85 knots is recommended. The advantage of this approach is that visual contact with the runway is easily maintained throughout.

Halfway around, bank away quickly to check for traffic on other approaches then resume the turn to the runway. If judged correctly, you straighten up just as its time to commence the landing flare when the runway disappears from view. From then on use peripheral vision, looking out both sides simultaneously to maintain the runway centerline. Basically, if you can see the runway then you are not over it!

Having achieved the correct nose attitude just above the ground with the engine idling, hold the stick right there. Perhaps, if you were more experienced with the Pitts, I would expand on that statement, but that will get you on the ground pretty well. Since most pilots step up to a Pitts from a Decathlon, they will need to unlearn the action of progressively moving the stick aft during the flare. That attitude is very important, so learn it well while on the ground before your first flight. It is also important enough to repeat that, if you do not get that exact three-point attitude, then have the nose a touch higher to drag the tail wheel gently on and let the mains sink on afterwards.

In Australia, we need to approach with at least a 500-meter, straight final leg so, in order to see the runway, the solution is to sideslip all the way down final until the flare is commenced. It is pretty obvious where to look as you can only see the runway on the opposite side from where you have pointed the nose.

Be alert to other traffic, however, which means checking what may be on the other side of the raised wing and what may be on the ground behind the cowl just waiting to taxi onto the runway as you reach short final. In the model S-2A, 80 knots is a good speed, reducing to 70 over the fence.

In a slight crosswind, point the nose into the wind so that the downwind wing is down in the sideslip—it makes for smaller angles of bank. Ten knots of crosswind seems ideal for a Pitts on a straight approach at 80 knots as the crab angle required is just enough to permit the runway to be viewed alongside the long, wide cowl with little sideslip.

At the last stage, you cancel the sideslip and convert the approach to the standard crosswind wing-down technique for the flare with a tail-low touchdown. It is the same nose attitude but, perhaps, allow the upwind main wheel to touch first or all three wheels together. Then pin all three wheels on the ground (back stick and into-wind aileron). The Pitts is very responsive and compact, aerodynamically speaking. So, anyone familiar with the type will not really be bothered by strong crosswinds up to the recommended maximum of 17 knots. When I do a Pitts checkout for a pilot, I ensure that we spend at least an hour flying patterns in crosswinds of around 15 knots.

I can remember when the Russian aerobatic team visited us in Australia with their Yak 50 and Sukhoi 26, back in 1986. They turned up one extremely windy morning to see our Pitts S-2A sitting there, firmly tied down. They could not believe that I had flown it in just a little earlier that morning in such a stiff crosswind.

Landing Roll

Once firmly on the ground, progressively bring the stick fully back to pin the tail wheel on the ground. If this is not done, your instructor will just sit there, jaw clamped tight to avoid jarring it, and watching the stick move as a result of each bounce on the ground, the stick movement aggravating the bounce—get the idea? It just keeps bouncing down the runway, admittedly feeling a lot worse from inside the cockpit than it looks from the outside.

The final stage of the landing is now upon us. Having slowed down somewhat, we lose the natural aerodynamic stability and rudder authority. If it is going to swing left or right, this is when it will happen, and quickly. Once you develop an intimate relationship with the airplane, you will feel this point as a definite reduction in directional stiffness. My best advice is, if you keep it straight, it will not swing, but I guess that statement needs further explanation. The tail wheel has now become the primary directional control. If you have the airplane pointed straight down the runway and, if you keep the tail wheel aligned with the airplane, then it will continue to track straight down the centerline.

You are probably thinking that this is a circular argument so I will continue. Keep ahead of the airplane by early reaction to any deviation from a straight landing roll and make small corrections early rather than making large corrections after the airplane has started a swing.

Anticipation is the key. A small deviation, with limited rudder deflection to correct it, will retain the tail wheel aligned with the airplane's longitudinal axis. Once you allow the tail wheel to turn, either by excessive departure from the intended direction, or driven by your rudder movement, the aircraft will immediately swing.

Further Comment

Most of the S-2As are without aileron counter-balances (spades). If you are lucky enough to fly a Pitts with spades, be especially wary of any bank near the ground or of letting a wheel lift off the ground after a crosswind landing or takeoff. There just is not that much clearance for the spade when you deflect the aileron to correct for it.

Another pointer on those later-model S-2As: the ground angle is higher (12° versus 9°) so do not try to land it like the other S-2As.

Pilots should become comfortable with the curving approach as it is a good option in a forced landing situation. Pick the field that is right on the wing tip, start the turn and just point it towards where you want to land.

Finally, some essential advice: a Pitts has sufficient power and control authority to fly away from any situation. If you have any problems, just go around for another attempt. With these notes, I did not intend to cover all the elements of a proper dual check. It is important to obtain proper instruction in this airplane as even very experienced pilots have come to grief with the type.

When I say instruction, I am not just referring to the landing. The Pitts is a beautiful airplane to fly, surprisingly docile in many respects in the air, but it also has other characteristics best learned with an experienced instructor. Just a word of warning: even experienced Pitts pilots can be seduced into becoming overconfident in their ability to master it. As the lady said, "love me, but respect me too!"

Chapter 22

Slepcev Storch

By David Robson

General Description

The Slepcev Storch is a three-quarter scale version of the famous Fieseler Storch observation and liaison airplane used by the Luftwaffe in World War II. It had incredible short-field performance due to its full-span Handley Page fixed slats, trailing-edge slotted flaps and a long, spindly landing gear, which allowed touchdown at an incredible angle of attack and low airspeed.

The legs place the main wheels well forward to the extent that the tail wheel is not just for balancing. It is a major working element of the supporting landing gear. It takes a strong person to lift the tail on the ground.

The Storch is the ultimate image of a functional airplane. It does what it was designed to do, without compromise to looks or style. It is functionally beautiful because of the the German design school, the Bauhaus, which promoted one prime rule of good design: form follows function. (The shape and appearance of the object should reflect the purpose of its design not the other way around; that is, design the vehicle to do the job not to look pretty. Remember the Volkswagon? The Storch is a flying Volkswagon, but even more efficient.)

The Slepcev version is a two-seat, tandem airplane with the same incredible short field performance. Added to the aerodynamic considerations is the need for a powerful, lightweight engine, as the landing performance must be matched by the takeoff performance, and the slowest possible landing speed is achieved with a high degree of induced lift from the propeller slipstream; that is, it occurs at quite high power. In the Storch replica, the tail wheel assembly is from the rugged Maule bush plane. The Slepcev Storch is powered by the Rotax four-stroke in either normal or turbocharged versions. Two-position slotted flap (up or down) are used for normal takeoff and landing.

Cockpit Ergonomics

The flap lever is in the upper left side of the cockpit roof. It has a button on the end to release the lock. It is awkward to operate and would be great if it functioned in the same way as the old handbrake lever. The equivalent of the mixture control would be full rich in the rearward position, which would be a little unusual.

Flight Operations

Preflight

The Storch is a conventional high-wing airplane as far as general inspection is concerned. Entry to the cockpit takes some special articulation of the pilot's body but, once settled inside, the cockpit is roomy and comfortable. The seat is not adjustable, nor are the rudder pedals, and my long legs caused me to consciously lift the balls of my feet to avoid inadvertently depressing the brake pedals.

Starting

Engine start is straightforward and, unusually, the stick is not held back (which is anathema to this taildragger pilot), but the Storch has such forward main wheels and long tail moment that there is a considerable weight on the tail wheel even when the aircraft is empty. Try lifting the tail by its handle: it takes a large person some considerable effort.

Taxiing

Taxiing is easy and the view forward is good from the front seat. The stick is held forward to reduce the weight on the tail wheel while taxiing. The brake levers above the rudder bar require the pilot's toes to be consciously lifted off the brakes while taxiing, but it is difficult to lift the foot so far.

Takeoff

Full forward stick is required as the throttle is opened fully. (There is a five-minute limit on maximum RPM.) The tail comes up and, very soon after, the wing comes alive and the aircraft wants to transition from wheels to wings. It is airborne in a ground roll of a few tens of yards and, with a 15-knot headwind, a few tens of feet. There is no need to look for airspeed or plan a conventional rotation. The aircraft tells you when to apply slight back pressure and leave the earth behind.

It then goes up like the proverbial elevator. It climbs at around 800 fpm with two on board, and the climb path is steep even though the aircraft's attitude is reasonable. However, like any ultralight, it has low inertia and high drag. It needs power for performance and for control: any loss of power requires an immediate lowering of the nose to maintain flying speed.

General Handling

The Storch has large ailerons, for low-speed roll control, and also marked adverse aileron yaw, which is easily countered by the very powerful rudder. The pilot's feet will be needed to balance the airplane with rudder input. Roll rate is surprisingly brisk if large coordinated aileron rudder inputs are made. There is little trim change with flap extension or power changes. However, the change in elevator control power with propeller slipstream (due to power) is most noticeable.

The airplane is stable and, surprisingly, rides turbulence well. The trim lever is small but powerful, and user-friendly.

The aircraft stalls between 25 and 15 KIAS depending on the power setting. It will not stall at all with power off and a single pilot in the front seat. There is not enough up elevator to raise the aircraft to the stalled angle of attack. Power (propeller slipstream) gives that control power, but this is not an airplane that could be accidentally stalled unless you had high power and aft CG. Stalling is a very deliberate maneuver in the Storch. There was no obvious tendency to drop a wing at the stall.

The Storch is not a speedster. It flies comfortably at 60 knots and equally so at 40 knots, but it is not in a hurry to go anywhere. It simply is not designed to.

The view is incredible and the response to gusts is surprisingly benign. It is a pleasant cruising airplane. This a great airplane for low-altitude surveillance.

Approach and Landing

The approach and landing can be described in a single word: stunning. The Storch is the first fixed-wing aircraft I have flown where you can totally disregard the airspeed indicator on final approach. You fly by feel and power. It is like a helicopter. The forward speed is almost irrelevant. You slow until below 35 knots, when the Storch shudders and its whole character changes. In the approach, there are two different Storches: one is a conventional airplane, the other is a kite. You can think of it as two different approaches: one conventional and, the other, hovering.

The conventional airspeed-referenced approach is flown at 45 knots with normal control inputs and technique. For the hovering approach, the aircraft is slowed nose-high until it tells you by a little shudder that it is now in its hover mode. The elevator holds attitude and power controls the path. The rate of descent and airspeed are largely irrelevant. The pilot drives the near-vertical approach path to the threshold and prepares to cushion the rate of descent with a marked burst of power, or to lower the nose and accelerate to 45 knots for a conventional landing. This transition takes some height and should not be left too late. The aircraft, remember, is increasing its speed by a 50 percent margin!

It is wise to leave some power on during the flare to keep the elevators breathing fresh air and then, after the aircraft levels and slows to a near stop, full back stick is reached quite quickly and the aircraft touches as soon as the power is reduced. There is no bounce: the 10-inch stroke of the spindly legs absorbs any remaining vertical velocity. It sits and stays. There is little tendency to divert into a ground loop as there is simply no energy left. The airplane is down and stopped in a few feet.

Because of the very steep approach path there is a massive attitude change in the flare, being around 20° (compared to 3° for a conventional airplane). The landing roll is virtually non-existent, again a few tens of feet.

Take careful note of the situation for the power-off glide and landing, whether for practice or for real. The Storch needs power for control of rate of descent and for elevator effect. In the event of a power-off approach the pilot needs to maintain at least 45 knots—I would recommend 50 knots—so that there is enough excess lift available to flare. As a result, the landing roll is longer than from a STOL approach.

Crosswind

The Storch has a demonstrated crosswind limit of 15 knots. This is a very real limit: the wing will lift, and full aileron will not stop it. It is better to land across the strip (under control), or approach along the centerline and yaw the aircraft flatly into wind before touchdown. It will then simply stop dead in a few feet.

Conclusion

As a youngster I dreamed of, and wondered why there was not, an airplane that would simply fly slower and slower until it could descend like a kite under full control. This would be the ultimate safe aircraft: just slow to a hover, and then enter a controlled near-vertical descent to a safe landing. Well, here it is. The Storch does this maneuver exactly.

It is quite remarkable. The aircraft, as it slows past 35 knots or so, changes its character completely. It shudders a little and becomes a vertically descending, powered kite. It hovers into-wind like a stalking hawk and can either swoop or kite to the ground. I use the term *kite* because that is exactly how it feels. The aircraft is held against the wind by thrust and the attitude is held level. Power adjustments then hover the aircraft and control its near-vertical descent. Yet it always feels safe and fully under control. Astounding and outstanding are both conservative descriptions. This is one hell of an airplane. I love it.

Chapter 23

Southern Cross Replica

By Captain Tom Russel

General Description

The Southern Cross Replica is a full-size replica of a 1926 Fokker Tri-motor, the F.VIIB-3m. It is an airplane built almost exactly to the drawings and specifications of the original Fokker Tri-motor. I say *almost exactly* because the same engines were not available and have been replaced by U.S. Jacobs radials. The original Southern Cross was the well-known aircraft flown on many pioneering flights by the great Aussie aviator Sir Charles Kingsford-Smith.

The Southern Cross Replica was constructed at Parafield, South Australia. Dimensions and form of the original aircraft have been maintained, although the engineering, avionics and crew communication systems are designed to modern standards. Safe ground handling required the replacement of the tail skid with a steerable/lockable tail wheel similar to the DC-3 aircraft.

This high-wing, light transport airplane is powered by three Jacobs R755-A2MI seven-cylinder radial engines mounted in the traditional way: left side (no. 1), center (no. 2), and right side (no. 3). Other aircraft of similar design were the Stinson Tri-motor, Ford Tri-motor (which flew to the North Pole), Junkers 52, and the de Havilland D.H.66 Hercules.

Flight Operations

Introduction

In the standard configuration the aircraft has a fuel capacity of 337 gallons in four tanks. Flight plan consumption is 42 gallons per hour at a true airspeed (TAS) of 90 knots. Practical endurance is six hours with reserves.

For a ferry flight, the aircraft can be fitted with an extra 119-gallon tank mounted in the cabin. Endurance then becomes 8 hours 30 minutes at a not-so-quick speed of 85 to 90 knots. (During the test flight program, in strong wind conditions, we were actually passed by a Volkswagen Beetle.)

Because of knobs and bolts on the rear cockpit bulkhead, the safety authority decided that military-style flying helmets must be worn. This also allowed the crew to utilize a hot mike intercom system to reduce the noise in the cockpit. (The cockpit is open-sided and those three Jacob radials are within six feet of the crew's ears.)

Preflight

While actual flying of the aircraft is very similar to the DC-3, the pretakeoff routine is more involved. A typical preflight starts about an hour before scheduled departure. First the crew needs to remove the oil collectors beneath each engine and to remove all of the control surface chocks.

The exterior preflight requires a ladder to get to the top of the wing to dip the fuel tanks, and then to cross-check the fuel sight-gauges in the cockpit.

The wing is a plywood-skinned, fabric-covered structure that requires some care.

The walk-round is standard with the added check of the flying control wires, all of which are visible along the outside of the fuselage and wing.

A check of the oil is essential before each flight and at each turn around. Similar to other aircraft of its vintage, oil consumption is an indication of engine health.

Starting

Prestart procedure includes an added check: the propeller of each engine must be pulled through by hand to avoid hydraulic lock (where the oil settles overnight and pools in the bottom cylinders of the radial engine). The oil is dispersed by manually rotating the propeller to circulate the oil; otherwise, there is an extreme pressure build-up on start, with possible engine damage.

Startup usually produces large clouds of blue smoke. After start, there is a lengthy period of time to allow the engines to warm up.

Taxiing

Taxiing the Fokker is a unique skill. The use of asymmetric power and the balanced use of the tail wheel lock are essential parts of the ground handling curriculum. To turn the aircraft, first unlock the tail wheel by pulling the lever up. This disengages the lock and allows the tail wheel to caster.

Now start your turn using brake and add power if necessary. Control the rate of turn and anticipate the point at which you apply opposite brake (to allow the tail wheel to trail so you can release the tail wheel lever to the locked position). The DC-3 has a similar arrangement.

Takeoff

Takeoff is conventional in that the tail wheel is left on the ground until about 25 knots and then the tail is raised gently to the level attitude. Keeping straight is by use of the rudder and by judicious use of asymmetric power in the initial run.

At about 55 knots, ease back on the control column to about a 6° or 7° nose-up attitude, allow the speed to build up to 70 knots, adjust the attitude and climb at that speed. Climb power is then set.

The aircraft has poor directional stability and the nose tends to slowly cycle left and right in normal flight. To keep straight, a recommended technique is to visually pick a point and line up the top cylinder of the front engine on that point. The aircraft gently oscillates around that point and, as long as the cylinder top comes back to your point, you are going straight. The compass is also suitable once you get used to the gentle left and right oscillation. You tend to average it out.

Cruise

In the cruise, the aircraft is stable, but requires a continuous check of the cylinder-head temperatures and attitude.

While it has a full set of instrumentation, pilots need to revert to the basic skills of stick and rudder. Precise balance, attitude control and trim are essential. The control column is a continuous wheel with a knot on the top to show when the column is centered.

While the Southern Cross is a VFR aircraft, it is fitted with ADF, VOR and, for longer trips, GPS. All of these modern systems make flying relatively straightforward, but the crews learned, usually the hard way, that visual flying in the outback or around the Blue Mountains (west of Sydney) required learning some old tricks of the trade.

The Open Cockpit

One important lesson was in cockpit organization; for example, stowing maps and charts where you could get to them, and where they would not get soaked in the rain nor disappear over the side. We found that we had to fold charts in such a way that they were narrow enough to hold securely, or we had to reinvent the old style roller-map holder. For those who remember open cockpits, nothing more needs to be said.

For those who do not, allow me to educate you. The opening up of a WAC or sectional chart tempted the wind in the cockpit to remove a significant portion of your chart from your hands and spread it over the land below. The missing portion is usually the one you desperately need.

On one memorable day, this happened over very mountainous terrain, at low level, with terrible weather, and when the GPS and VOR decided to take a vacation! ATC could not help because our wooden structure did not give a good radar return. So, essentially, it was back to the 1920s.

The weather was truly atrocious and we were also aware that we were in charge of the only flying replica of the Southern Cross, which had cost a million dollars to build. We were also in the area in which the sister ship of the original Southern Cross, the Southern Cloud, had gone missing many years before.

Most Southern Cross flight crews had been airline pilots with a background in tail wheel aircraft in their early days. However, at this time, most of us were in command of RPT jet aircraft with modern avionics and navigation systems.

Visual navigation, at low level in rain, with low cloud and with carburetor icing, were not part of our normal workday routine. However, the old skills were there, a little rusty perhaps, but usable.

To cut a long story short, we safely landed to be greeted by a line-up of international jets waiting for air traffic control to get us out of the way!

General Handling

Control forces are heavy compared to modern aircraft, but not uncomfortably so. Turns are relatively stable, but require conscious rudder input to maintain balance. Crews rapidly adjusted to turns without using the bat-and-ball or turn-and-slip by the very old method of wind on your cheeks.

Unbalanced, there is a noticeable draft on your cheek in the direction of unbalance, whereas balanced, there is no wind. Angle of bank was set by using the position of the top three cylinders on the front engine.

Stalling is docile. The stall is positive, although no airframe buffet is noted. Recovery is standard. We found in training that the application of power and a slight reduction in the nose attitude would result in a climb away from the stall. The stall speed was about 30 knots indicated airspeed. However, there was a significant position error. It was decided, after testing, that 45 knots IAS was the actual figure.

Approach and Landing

The pattern, approach and landing are not complicated, but there are some essentials to be considered.

Downwind, your spacing should be the same as any other aircraft you fly, with the wing tip tracking down the centerline of the runway. How, though, in this high-wing aircraft, do you get orientated? Simple. You line up the runway along the top of the engine nacelle. This puts you at the right spacing.

Normal prelanding checks are carried out and your base turn is at the standard 45° to the threshold. A gentle reduction of power, lower the nose and maintain 70 knots. Retrim. Because the aircraft has no flaps, the approach is flatter than you are used to. On final approach, reduce your speed to be at the threshold at 60 knots.

Close the power levers as you flare to a level or slightly nose-up attitude. Allow the aircraft to gently sink on to the ground in the wheeler attitude.

Once on the ground, apply gentle forward pressure to hold the aircraft on the ground in the level attitude until about 30 knots when the tail wheel can be gently lowered to the ground.

Because of the main wheel design, which has a degree of inward cant, it is possible to scuff the tires if brakes are applied too soon before the full weight of the aircraft is on them. If you try to lower the tail too soon, the aircraft tries to fly again.

Once on the ground and clear of the runway, taxiing the aircraft is as before.

With the knowledge that the original aircraft had landed in fields the size of a football ground, some testing took place and we found that an approach speed of 50 knots could be achieved with a significant reduction in landing distance. This type of approach requires tight control of approach path and airspeed and is not recommended for routine line flying.

Conclusion

The Southern Cross replica flew around Australia and New Zealand on several occasions. The biggest negative factor was weather. The crosswind limit of 15 knots was tested on several occasions and only served to prove that only pilots with considerable tail wheel experience should fly the aircraft.

Index